Compliments
of

**Dr. Janet
Hoskins**
Warden &
Vice-Chancellor
St John's College

St. John's College

St. John's College

Faith and Education
in Western Canada

J.M. Bumsted

University of Manitoba Press

University of Manitoba Press
Winnipeg, Manitoba R3T 2M5 Canada
www.umanitoba.ca/uofmpress

Printed in Canada on acid-free paper.

Cover and text design: Doowah Design
Cover photograph: St. John's College Theological Group 1927-1928 (detail)
Title page: A.B. Adamson (captain, St. John's College football team 1907-1908)

Library and Archives Canada Cataloguing in Publication

Bumsted, J. M., 1938-
   St. John's College : faith and education in Western Canada / Jack M. Bumsted.

Includes bibliographical references and index.

ISBN 0-88755-692-2
   1. St. John's College (Winnipeg, Man.)—History. I. Title.

LE3.S56272B84 2006   378.7127'43   C2006-905051-1

The University of Manitoba Press gratefully acknowledges the financial support for its publication program provided by the Government of Canada through the Book Publishing Industry Development Program (BPIDP), the Canada Council for the Arts, the Manitoba Arts Council, and the Manitoba Department of Culture, Heritage, and Tourism.

TABLE OF CONTENTS

Photographs appear between pages 74 and 75 and pages 154 and 155.

To the Johnians in my family.

Preface

ONE OF THE MANY THINGS I LEARNED WHILE DOING THE RESEARCH for *The University of Manitoba: An Illustrated History* was just how rich were the archives of St. John's College. I relied on them extensively for the early chapters of the university's history, and I was therefore quite amenable to taking on a historical project for St. John's College. Kathryn Young asked me to assume responsibility for a work that had begun life earlier as a collection of anecdotal memoirs by those associated with it, paralleling a similar book recently published by St. Paul's College. I was not much interested in centring a book around anecdotes, but I offered instead to use them as illustrative documents for a new history of the college. I had in mind neither a celebratory romp through the past nor a huge tome with several hundred pages of footnotes. I had several examples of the latter sitting on my shelves. At the outset, I knew just enough about the background of the history of the college to know that the archival material would sustain a complex story, and I hoped that, if presented without superscripts and the usual scholarly trappings, an audience of old Johnians and other readers interested in the lives of small institutions of higher learning might find the account interesting and instructive. A biography of the college, therefore, was what I intended from the beginning, and what has come out in the end.

As I did the research and writing for this book, I became increasingly aware that none of the usual models for a church-related liberal arts college in the historical literature of higher education quite fit the St. John's College situation. Indeed, a major problem was that there was never a single model for a church-related liberal arts college in Britain, the United States, or Canada. St. John's College was structurally and administratively based, not on a generic Oxford College, but on Christ Church College, Oxford, with its intimate connection between college and cathedral chapter. On the other hand, St. John's College in its teaching replicated neither the tutorial system nor the tripos, but followed instead the Canadian pattern of lectures and course examinations. Furthermore, St. John's College at a very early stage of its development became a founding college within a university structure which, while mainly a virtual one before 1900, nevertheless altered the dynamic substantially. Bishop Machray wanted to situate St. John's within a university structure, but he was unable to control what this would mean. In any event, finding a standard model that could be understood and replicated was no easy matter for the early founders.

If St. John's College was in some respects *sui generis,* in other respects its history was quite representative of the problems of church-related higher education in Canada and especially in the prairie region of western Canada. The history of St. John's continually intersects with the development of Manitoba and prairie Canada over the 150 years since its founding. When Louis Riel led his Métis in righteous indignation against the government of Canada, Bishop Robert Machray was there, counselling moderation amongst the Protestant mixed bloods of the Red River Settlement. When Winnipeggers celebrated Queen Victoria's diamond jubilee in 1897, St. John's held a special ceremony. When Canada went to war in 1914, St. John's

College's students, alumni, and staff were in the front row of volunteers. When a major financial scandal in 1932 — the defalcation, as it is known — brought down the old boys' network in Winnipeg, the culprit held, among many other responsibilities, the office of bursar of St. John's College. The college's changing fortunes also paralleled those of the Anglican Church itself, particularly in Manitoba but by extension right across the West. Beginning as a missionary institution in the early nineteenth century, the college quickly became part of the WASP establishment of Winnipeg. It declined with that establishment after 1932 and then again in the 1960s with the triumph of secularism. But the college has not simply been an Anglican institution, but an educational one connected since the 1870s with the liberal arts in complex ways. Its history as a liberal arts college tells us much about the changing place of the arts disciplines in Manitoba and the Canadian West since the middle of the nineteenth century. Arts was initially subordinated to theology, then held an equal place with it, struggling to find local and external funding until ultimately both arts and theology declined in the face of occupationalism and instrumentalism in Canadian higher education.

As well as because of its central place in the history of Canadian education, the St. John's College story needs to be told for other reasons. In the first place, the archives are exceptionally rich, documenting in detail the development of the college from its earliest beginning 150 years ago. Few educational institutions in Canada, much less in western Canada, have the continuous record that St. John's College possesses, or one of such duration. St. John's was one of the first educational institutions in modern Canada founded west of southern Ontario, and it has been fortunate enough to have been able to preserve its records free from fire and other ravages of time. In the second place, the early history of St. John's College — like that of the other founding colleges of the University of Manitoba — forms an important and integral part of the history of the university. Before the establishment of the faculty of science at the University of Manitoba in 1904, institutions like St. John's College did the teaching at the university and were responsible for its extracurricular activities as well. Third, the history of St. John's College, particularly in more recent times, is not well understood by its own staff, students, and alumni. Much mythology has crept into the tale. This account tries to set the record straight on such mythical matters as the college's role in the founding of the university, its place in the defalcation of 1932, and its response to the agreement with the university in 1970. Finally, the story of St. John's College is an amazing illustration of tenacious institutional survival, of constant reinvention in the face of obstacles that would have cowed most organizations.

Finding a balance between too much and too little detail was one of the hardest parts of writing this book. In general, I have tried to keep the narrative moving and have avoided getting bogged down in too much descriptive material or the inclusion of too many names. My chief interest is in the overall dynamic of the college and the policies that governed it. Readers will notice that only the principal actors are provided with extensive biographical material, and most of the individuals included in the narrative are only briefly identified rather than described at length. To have taken any other approach would have meant a much longer and much different book. For similar reasons, I have tried to capture the flavour of student life in the various eras, but have not attempted to list every winning sports team or student achievement. A separate volume is needed to expand on my account — and take full advantage of the college archives — and I hope it will soon be undertaken.

Another difficult decision was how to handle the recent past. I decided to end my detailed narrative in 1980, only coincidentally because it was the year I joined the college. As I discovered in preparing the history of the university, portraying recent events is a problematic business, partly because they are difficult to put into perspective, particularly by a historian who is still living within the institution. Current faculty and staff will not only have their own understandings of what happened, but they will have an understandable interest in seeing that their bailiwick receives not only judicious treatment but an appropriate amount of attention. Readers will thus find the years after 1980 dealt with relatively briefly in an epilogue.

Finally, the question always arises about what standards are to be used in judging and assessing the behaviour of people in the past. On the whole, I have accepted the standards of the time, although I was often struck by the narrowness of vision of some of those involved in the St. John's College story, and occasionally have commented upon it. The defalcation was a crucial event and could not be avoided, and I have tried to face up to it squarely without trepidation. The agreement of 1970 was another more recent turning point in the college's history, and I have tried to understand it in the light of conditions and thinking at the time.

What has struck me most about those who were part of the St. John's College story is their indomitable faith in the rightness of the enterprise, even when everything was collapsing around them. It is that faith that has sustained the college over the years.

Chapter One

The Precursors, 1820–1866

THE RED RIVER SETTLEMENT WAS FOUNDED BY LORD SELKIRK in 1812 at the forks of the Red and Assiniboine rivers. It was intended to serve both as a haven for redundant Highlanders and Irish and a retirement home for families in the fur trade, most of whom were of mixed-blood origin. By 1830 the latter intention was much more important than the former, and the settlement became the largest community of mixed-blood people in western North America. To the outside world it appeared to be a small, isolated, frontier community teetering precariously on the edge between civilization and savagery. This was the view presented by Alexander Ross in his book, *The Red River Settlement,* published in 1856. In some ways the perception was accurate. Physically, the settlement was isolated on the frontier. It was an island surrounded in every direction by hundreds of kilometres of land inhabited by First Peoples and a handful of fur traders. Travelling to Red River required a lengthy summer journey by water from Lake Superior, by water from Hudson Bay, or overland from the United States. Demographically, Red River was never numerically large. By the 1860s it contained about 13,000 inhabitants, including a few hundred Aboriginal people and a large population of French-speaking and English-speaking mixed-blood people.

Appearances were, in some senses, deceiving. Red River's inhabitants, especially the Métis, rapidly became linked to the capitalistic society of the United States through the medium of the Red River cart. Spiritually and intellectually, Red River's elite had long since become integrated into the outside world. It would have been no idle boosterism to maintain that, for its size and situation, by the 1860s Red River harboured one of North America's most lively and best-educated communities. The settlement had three choral societies. The Institute of Rupert's Land had been organized in 1862 to provide a forum for scientific and humanistic discussion. A subscription library of 2500 volumes flourished. Most of the leading fiction and non-fiction of the Victorian era were readily available in the library or in the bookstore operated by the proprietors of the local newspaper, *The Nor'-Wester*, established in 1859. British journals and newspapers were brought to Red River by a regular mail service, usually operated as an extension of the United States Post Office. Part of this lively intellectual life was the result of the early establishment of education in this remote settlement. The two denominations that had taken the lead in Red River were the Catholic and the Anglican churches.

The beginnings of formal institutions of education came to Red River in 1818, when three Catholic priests from Quebec—Frs. Provencher, Edge, and Dumoulin—arrived in the settlement on 16 July. These priests had been literally prised out of the grasp of the Bishop of Quebec by Lord Selkirk's people in Lower Canada, who insisted that without religion and education there would be no way to civilize the mixed bloods of the region. Those mixed bloods, not yet calling themselves Métis, had killed a number of settlers at the battle of Seven Oaks in 1816, and had opposed the settlement at every opportunity. A fundraising campaign had ensued, supported by Lower Canada's governor and various other officials recruited mainly through the charms of Lady Selkirk. Once in Red River, the priests began almost immediately building a house on the east side of the Red River, with a section, six by nine metres, finished by winter. The house, divided in half, served as chapel, residence, and schoolhouse. Children from the settlement began attending makeshift classes that autumn.

Two years later, the first Protestant clergyman arrived at York Factory. The Reverend John West was officially chaplain to the Hudson's Bay Company (HBC) at Red River, appointed by the company's London Committee in October 1819. Lord Selkirk had, from the beginnings of the recruitment of Highland settlers for Red River in 1811, promised a Presbyterian clergyman for the settlement. He had actually contracted with one in 1813, but the man had begged off at the last minute. West had sailed aboard the Eddystone on 27 May 1820 in company with a schoolmaster named George Harbidge. The two men arrived at York Factory on 14 August, and West submitted a plan for care and education of Indian schools to the governor of the HBC's Southern Department, William Williams. West had proposed that the mission school to be supported by the Church Missionary Society (CMS) might also educate a few children of the settlement, as well as the abandoned or orphaned children of country marriages between European traders and native women. This plan was eventually rejected by Governor George Simpson on grounds of expense. West nevertheless arranged at York Factory for an Aboriginal boy (later named James Hope) to join him at Red River. At Norway House he added another boy, the Swampy Cree orphan who would become Henry Budd. He later recruited Thomas Hassall and Charles Pratt as additional students. West had come to Red River under the understanding that he would bring Christianity to the Aboriginal peoples, and from the beginning he made missionary activity among the First Peoples his major priority.

In September 1821, Nicholas Garry, one of Lord Selkirk's trustees, while at York Factory—on his way back from the settlement, which he had visited on behalf of the HBC—had presided at the formation of an auxiliary of the Bible Society by John West. Garry wrote, "the Readiness which was shown by every Gentleman to subscribe proves how erroneous the Opinions of

People have been that there was no Religion in the Country. I subscribed £50 for the Hudson Bay Company and the whole amount was £130, which when the few Gentlemen assembled is considered, was a large sum." In July 1822, West opened a building intended for a schoolhouse and temporary place of worship; it had "apartments for the schoolmaster, accommodation for the Indian children, a day-school for the children of the settlers." The building was also intended to serve as a church, and West first used the edifice to baptize two of his wards, James Hope and Henry Budd. George Harbidge was the first schoolmaster, but he turned out to be a drunk and couldn't teach arithmetic and was soon replaced.

The two educational establishments begun so early in the life of the colony—the Catholic and the Anglican—would reflect the religious development of the Red River Settlement throughout its existence. The settlement itself was an isolated island of population surrounded by wilderness and First Peoples for almost 2400 kilometres in any direction. By 1830 the bulk of the population of Red River would be composed of mixed-blood people, the sons and daughters of European fur traders, and Aboriginal women born in the country, who replaced earlier European transplants—Scots, Germans, Swiss, Canadians, Norwegians—most of whom had fled the region's harsh climate and continual series of natural disasters, culminating with a great flood in 1826. Slightly over half the inhabitants of Red River would come to be composed of francophone Catholics, who were eventually known as Métis. The Catholics would be served by priests recruited mainly in French Canada, occasionally in France itself. Just under half the population would be made up of anglophone Protestants, most of them mixed-blood people from the HBC trading posts and adherents of the Church of England, which supplied a constant stream of missionaries, usually under the auspices of the Church Missionary Society. Although many Catholic and Protestant clergymen were sent to the West to minister to the First Nations, those who remained resident in the settlement tended to concentrate on the European and mixed-blood populations.

In 1823 John West was replaced by the Reverend David Jones and the schoolmaster by William Garrioch, an Orkneyman long employed by the HBC. A farm was established next to the building to provide employment for the students and fresh produce for the table. Before long William Cockran, who joined Jones as a missionary in 1825, was clearly in charge of both the farm and the school. Cockran attempted to supervise student labour on the farm, but observed, "as soon as I leave the little fellows they turn their backs on work." His charges were obviously not very keen students. Cockran taught using one of the then fashionable monitorial systems of instruction:

> Very often when I am asking the children at the head of the class some questions, those at the back drop asleep, and the first intelligence I have of it is from their sonorous nostrils snuffing the air, or from their Bibles falling upon the floor.

A few day students were apparently in the classroom as well, but the missionaries felt the need for both a residential school and a female school. Cockran's wife was employed in 1827 to teach females, and by 1829 had eighteen female students. Neither of the Cockrans was happy with their situation, however. In 1831 Cockran told Governor Simpson that he could not afford the expense of repairing and heating the schoolroom, adding that "the few children sent by the [HBC] officers" were not sufficient to require Mrs. Cockran's exclusive services.

The Reverend David Jones established the Red River Academy in 1833 at Upper Church. When it merged with another privately owned boarding school, one managed by the early settler John Pritchard, the academy became the sole source of secondary education available for the Protestant community in the Northwest. Through the aid of Hudson's Bay Company governor George Simpson, Jones enrolled seventeen boys and sixteen girls in his two-storey wooden structure. It consisted of two wings joined by a covered walkway. Jones undertook the post of headmaster while his wife supervised the girls until her untimely death in 1836. The curriculum offered to boys and girls was the usual one of the time. It was described in a report to the Church Missionary Society in 1835: "The course of instruction for the young ladies' school embraces reading, writing, arithmetic, geography, the use of globes, history, and catechetical information. In the young gentlemen's school progress is made in reading, writing, arithmetic, bookkeeping, algebra, mathematics, Latin, Greek, &c. The younger ones read *Delectus* and study grammar, history, &c., while the newcomers are in the New Testament and Catechisms of various sorts." Despite the impressive "course of instruction," the schoolmasters seemed most proud of "the proper marriages made by the young ladies, who, being raised from their former condition will take the station the female ought at all times to occupy in society." Their first success was Sarah MacLeod, who married John Ballenden and would later become the centre of a major Red River scandal and notorious court case.

John Macallum, an MA graduate from King's College, Aberdeen, was hired as an instructor in 1833 (and was later ordained on the visit of Bishop George Mountain of Montreal to the settlement in 1844). Macallum's strong educational background provided an emphasis on a classical education. With Reverend Jones still mourning the death of his wife and returning to England, the reins of the academy were turned over to Macallum in 1837. Many former students of the academy went on to prominent posts within the Hudson's Bay Company. William and Henry Hardisty both became chief factors and William McMurray became an inspecting factor. The most noteworthy scholar educated at the academy, however, was Alexander Kennedy Isbister, a mixed-blood man born at Cumberland House. The recipient of an MA from Edinburgh University, Isbister became the author of many books and secretary of the Aborigines Protection Society, the chief private organization concerned with Aboriginal policy in the British Empire. Following Isbister's death in 1887, much of his fortune was left to institute the Isbister Scholarship Fund in Manitoba, and the University of Manitoba still awards Isbister scholarships.

While the Reverend Macallum may have been a decent classical scholar, he was much better known in Red River as a fierce disciplinarian, a red-wigged snuff taker who believed that corporal punishment "invigorates both the body & mind of the pupil, and implants & cherishes habits which will be of essential service in active life." Macallum dealt out his invigoration with a "finger-sized native brown willow stick, about three and half feet long." He would not be the last of the floggers. In 1841 Macallum purchased the school for £350, and reported great satisfaction with the behaviour of his students. Letitia Hargrave in York Factory had, via the HBC's rumour mill, a rather different impression of Macallum's success:

> They say that Mr Macallum's school is going to wreck. Children who have had duck, geese & venison 3 times a day are supposed to suffer from breakfasts of milk & water with dry bread, severe floggings, confinement after any fault & the total want of the following meal. The boys & girls are constantly fainting but Macallum won't change his system. Many girls have got ill, and as he makes them strip off their Indian stockings & adopt English fashions it is not surprising. They must take a certain walk every day, plunging thro' the freezing snow. They wear Indian shoes, but without the cloth stockings or leggins [leggings] over them. The snow gets in & I need not say that the feelings one undergoes are not comfortable.

Not surprisingly, Macallum's student numbers began to fall off in the face of "a current of unfavourable opinion" consisting chiefly of what the headmaster described as "misrepresentations, calumnies, and declensions." By 1848 both Macallum and his school were in ill health, and the headmaster died in 1849 on the same day that Bishop David Anderson, the first bishop, arrived in Red River. Anderson brought with him a resolution of the Committee of Correspondence of the CMS that £500 be apportioned from the Jubilee Fund for a "Church missionary Seminary in Rupert's Land for the education and training of native teachers." Anderson took over the academy, and moved personally to the academy grounds at Upper Church in Kildonan.

It is clear that there was continuity between John Macallum's Red River Academy and the newly named "St. John's Collegiate School" and "St. John's College." The first written records surviving of St. John's Collegiate School are in the college archives, dating from 1850. A series of resolutions established a board for the school, and dealt with a number of papers submitted to the board. The first paper was concerned with the bishop's residence, which had been purchased from Adam Thom, the first "recorder" (or judge) of Red River, and renamed "Bishop's Court." A note added here observed that a portrait of James Leith had been procured. It was the estate of James Leith, an HBC fur trader, that had provided the money for the founding of the bishopric. The second paper dealt with the establishment of "St. John's Collegiate School," which was intended to instruct the young and, in a "higher Department," prepare catechists and candidates for the ministry.

From the outset, therefore, a seminary offering education beyond the secondary level was envisaged and was even in precarious existence, although the documents admitted that "the erection of a College on a larger scale, as in many Colonial Dioceses, has been found impracticable." In his *Charge Delivered to the Clergy of the Diocese of Rupert's Land, at his Primary Visitation* (delivered in 1850 and published in London in 1851), Bishop Anderson foresaw new buildings for St. John's Cathedral, the collegiate school, and "as a part of it, at present and hereafter, it may be a separate building, would be the institution for the training of a native ministry, St. John's College." The third paper dealt with scholarships, which were intended to "assimilate St. John's College as far as possible, with kindred institutions whether in Colonial Dioceses or in the Mother Country." The fourth paper established a library for the use of the board, the clergy of the diocese, and the scholars of St. John's. J.S. Clouston and Henry Budd were appointed joint librarians. It also provided for listing the books, which was done in a separate catalogue.

Some of the student body of the new school whose names have been recorded went on to higher education in other places, chiefly to Cambridge and to the University of Toronto. Such students were clearly enrolled in the collegiate school. But other students receiving instruction, such as John Chapman, W.H. Taylor, Henry Budd, and Thomas Cockran, were equally clearly candidates for the priesthood. They appear to have been taught separately, at least part of the time, by Bishop Anderson. In 1852 Cockran—a candidate for the diaconate—wrote two examinations and was required to sketch the outline of a sermon. He subsequently served as college tutor and master of the collegiate school until 1859. Over the years eight natives of the HBC's Western Territories and several British-born newcomers were instructed at Anderson's "college" prior to their ordination. In 1858 Bishop Anderson, in his charge to the clergy of his diocese, wrote:

> And yet I feel that the very name of the college may at times perplex and bewilder from the scanty number which we can assemble in this land, and the little claim that we can make to anything approaching to college life. But as I think of and use the word, I revert to bygone years, and the meaning of the term in early years. In this sense I would employ it, as embracing not the pupils and scholars alone, but the Bishop and clergy also, forming a missionary college in a dark land. I would regard each clergyman as a member of that college, and it thus becomes a centre uniting us all.

As Anderson acknowledged in this passage, St. John's College was rather more a "virtual" college than an institution with a hard physical presence. As such, it would be more difficult to dissolve than the collegiate school, which was closed in 1859 after years of "heavy pecuniary loss." The non-physical college described by Bishop Anderson continued, chiefly in the form of its library, which later served as the early basis for the library in the college founded by Bishop Machray in 1866.

A St. John's College had existed in Red River in the 1850s. As good a case could have been made out for dating the establishment of St. John's College from 1850 as could be advanced for 1866, the date commonly used for the founding.* Bishop Machray always operated as though the college he founded was something new in Red River, totally ignoring the provenance of some of the books in the new St. John's College library. Whether established in 1850 or in 1866, St. John's College and the Catholic school at St. Boniface were both mainly concerned with pre-university education. Nevertheless, they provided a significant element of culture to a wilderness community.

---

* I have been unable to establish when the college took 1866 as its founding date.

Chapter Two

A Theological College, 1866–1876

BETWEEN THE LATE 1860S AND THE MID-1870S, enormous changes occurred in Red River. As one of its first actions, the newly unified nation of Canada purchased the vast territories of the Hudson's Bay Company (including Red River), and attempted to create an internal empire in the northwestern part of North America. The inhabitants of Red River, led by the Métis, resisted this takeover. The insurgents, led by Louis Riel, succeeded in forcing Canada to negotiate the admission of Red River into Confederation as a separate, albeit small, province called Manitoba. New settlers began trickling into Manitoba from Great Britain and Canada (Ontario and, to a lesser extent, Quebec). Winnipeg was established as a city in 1873, and its leaders were, from the beginning, active in "boosting" both the city and the surrounding province. St. John's College under the direction of Bishop Robert Machray was an important part of early Winnipeg's cultural infrastructure. Because of the early religious history of Manitoba, the Anglican

Church was an important denomination from the beginning of extensive settlement.

On 25 June 1865 Robert Machray was consecrated in England as Bishop of Rupert's Land. Machray had been born in Aberdeen in 1831, the son of an advocate (or lawyer), and was baptized in the Church of Scotland, the reformed church created by John Knox in the sixteenth century. He grew up in the time of the Disruption; in 1843 the Church of Scotland split in two, with hundreds of ministers and congregations forming the Free Church of Scotland. Robert chose to remain with the Church of Scotland proper, although his biographer would later insist that he secretly preferred the Church of England. Many Aberdonian Presbyterians—including Bishop John Strachan of Upper Canada—shared this preference. Machray attended the Grammar School of Aberdeen in preparation for admission to Marischal College, but he eventually entered King's College in 1847. Here he came to excel in mathematics and acquired a bosom friend in the person of another Scots student, John McLean. Following graduation, Machray entered Sidney Sussex College at Cambridge in 1851, hoping that his previous success in mathematics would prove useful to him. Machray spent four years at Sidney College, and at the end he was ready to accept ordination in the Church of England. After a hiatus of several years and a visit to Italy, he returned to Sidney College as dean in 1858, undertaking parochial work in the Cambridge area in addition to his college duties. He was thus an ideal candidate for the post of bishop in the isolated, colonial diocese of Rupert's Land—young, energetic, experienced—and pledged himself before his departure overseas to three objects in his new diocese: encouraging an indigenous church; inducing each congregation to become self-supporting; and securing the dominance of the Church of England in the region.

Robert Machray was an impressive figure in the nineteenth-century Anglican Church in Canada. He was one of the church's greatest Canadian prelates; probably only Bishop John Strachan was his superior. Strachan dominated the first half of the nineteenth century; Machray dominated the second half. Like Strachan, Machray lived long and was in power for many years. He might perhaps be better known had his primary orbit of influence been in eastern Canada rather than the prairie West. Incalculable is the effect on his reputation created by the fact that his biographer—a nephew—produced a huge hagiographic tome almost a century ago, and then destroyed the personal papers on which it was based. By the time of Machray's appointment as bishop, it was clear that the Red River Settlement and the vast lands of the Hudson's Bay Company were soon going to be transferred to Canada. The achievement of a native church required, as Machray himself put it in a letter home in November 1865, that he "establish a College for the training of those who wish a better education, in the fear of God, in useful learning, and in conscientious attachment to our Church." As an educator, he had grown up in both the Scottish and the English universities, which he knew intimately, but was totally ignorant of North American systems and practices, either in the United States or Canada.

On 5 December 1865, Machray summoned all his clergy in the Red River Settlement to a meeting, which drew up a report of the state of the church in the diocese. In late May 1866, Machray again summoned his clergy—and this time lay delegates from his diocese—to attend a conference to plan for the future. After the celebration of divine service at the Cathedral, the conference "assembled in St. John's Schoolroom" and heard a lengthy address by the bishop, subsequently reprinted in London in a pamphlet. Machray reported on a variety of matters, including both his thinking and action on the matter of "a School of a more general character than a purely theological College." He observed that no school had replaced Macallum's academy, and he admitted that he had initially intended to establish a college, with separate programs in theology, classics, and mathematics. But he had subsequently abandoned a more general school and proposed instead simply a theological one. He had therefore invited the Reverend John McLean (who had been acting as a clergyman in London, Canada West) to become a theological tutor under the auspices of the Church Missionary Society. A mission tour over the winter of 1865–66 brought Machray back to his original plan, however, for "a College of theology and general education, to be called St. John's College." The bishop noted that this name would continue the name of Bishop Anderson's institution. Teaching would be in the hands of a warden and two masters, with Machray's own assistance. As warden he had John McLean, who had accepted the post and would be present in September. A short, stout man, McLean would physically provide a nice counterpoint to the bishop, who was tall and thin. As third master Machray hoped to obtain the services of Samuel Pritchard, another young schoolmaster, whose school in St. Andrews would be incorporated into the new venture.

In 1875 Machray told the Rupert's Land Synod that he had patterned St. John's after the theological schools of the great universities of Britain, each of which was connected with a cathedral church. The two models he named at this time were the cathedrals of Christ Church, Oxford, and Ely, near Cambridge. But it is not certain that this had been precisely his thinking ten years earlier, when the creation of new theological schools in Oxford and Cambridge had been a movement in its infancy. In any event, in 1874 Machray had encouraged the Manitoba legislature to incorporate the dean and chapter of St. John's Cathedral. He subsequently that same year made the professor of systematic theology a cathedral canon, and a year later the professor of exegetical theology and the professor of ecclesiastical history also became canons. The incumbents of the first two professorial cum canonical appointments—the Reverends John Grisdale and James Dallas O'Meara—were both long-standing faculty members at the college, Grisdale serving until he became Bishop of Qu'Appelle in 1896 and O'Meara until his death in 1901. Also in 1875, male children of members of the congregation of the cathedral were admitted to the collegiate school as day students at half fees. Machray continued to maintain a close connection between college and cathedral for the duration of his episcopate, and the relationship continued for many years thereafter.

In his May 1866 address to the synod, Machray offered his thoughts on a variety of other organizational matters, adding that the governing council of the college would make all such decisions. He wanted two classes of boarders, and day students who would pay four to six pounds per year for instruction. There would be two vacations, at Christmas and midsummer, with two terms of study of twenty weeks each. In the short run, the new institution would use existing facilities, including the surviving building of St. John's College or collegiate school, which would be raised and have a kitchen added. Machray had called a meeting of the remaining members of the collegiate board of Bishop Anderson's St. John's College, who reported that the college's assets consisted of some dilapidated buildings and the college library, housed at the bishop's residence. Machray told his listeners in May that this "valuable and well selected library" would become the basis for that of St. John's College, to which he had some other volumes to add. In his report to the second meeting of his clergy in May 1867, Machray added that not only did the new college retain the name of its predecessor, but it carried on "the most happy motto of the early institution—'In thy light shall we see light.'" The bishop subsequently noted that there was still £250 left in the Society for the Propagation of Christian Knowledge grant to "old St. John's College," which he hoped to apply to a building fund for new stone buildings. Here was further evidence that Bishop Anderson's endeavour had not completely disappeared, and that Machray's college was being built on its foundation.

The 1867 meeting was given considerable information about the progress of St. John's College, which had formally opened on 1 November 1866, in its first year. Machray reported that he had issued a constitution and a temporary body of statutes for governing the college. Enrolment had proven quite decent. There were three senior theological students, twenty-six pupils in the collegiate school, and seven junior theological students preparing for missionary work among the First Nations. Obviously there was no "Arts" college as such. The bishop insisted that the college was absolutely essential for the missionary thrust of the church, and therefore its funding was critical. He had contemplated sending the warden off to the United States to raise funds, but was advised against this visit by members of the American Episcopal Church because of the nation's "distracted condition"; the Civil War had only recently ended and reconstruction was still in progress. Nevertheless, some money had been raised in England. Existing buildings were completely occupied, and a new wooden building for classrooms would have to be built almost immediately. The Cockran Scholarship had raised over £330 in subscriptions, most of which had been invested in 5 percent Canadian government debentures. An appendix to the published report of the 1867 meeting reprinted the constitution and statutes of St. John's College, Rupert's Land, as well as an official report from the warden, dated 27 May 1867, which reported on current enrolment numbers. One additional document listed the boarding fees (twelve pounds to the warden per term, and ten pounds to the English master, students furnishing their own bedding and towels), and the tuition fees (£2.10 per term for day students and one pound per term for boarders). Within a few weeks of this 1867 gathering, the new nation of Canada began its existence, and less than six months later, began preparations for the purchase of Rupert's Land from the Hudson's Bay Company.

Most of what we know of the college in its earliest days comes from official reports and scraps of documents dealing mainly with other matters. The academic year was divided into two terms of twenty weeks each, beginning on 29 January and 1 August. Students were in class from 9:00 a.m. to 12:30 p.m. and from 1:30 p.m. to 3:00 p.m. Much of the teaching was done through the lecture system, which was combined with a good deal of memorization of information. The Oxbridge tutorial system was certainly not introduced into Red River in these early days, if it ever was. A good memory was an absolute essential to academic success. All students wrote examinations immediately before the midsummer and Christmas holidays. Boarders were expected to study from 6:30 to 7:30 a.m. and from 6:00 to 8:00 p.m. Surviving school regulations, read aloud to students at the outset of every term, suggest that the model was more an English public school than a university, hardly surprising, given the early clientele and focus of instruction. Indeed, Westminster School, at first unofficially and later more consciously, became the exemplar.

The first years of the college were a period of considerable turmoil for Red River. A famine in 1868 was followed soon after, in 1869, by the attempted takeover by Canada of the HBC territory. This resulted in the rebellion of 1869–70 led by Louis Riel and the admission in 1870 of Red River into Canada as the province of Manitoba. Although we have virtually no records of the college for these troubled years, one suspects there was considerable disruption of classes over the winter of 1869–70. Certainly Bishop Robert Machray and Warden John McLean played a considerable role in the events of the uprising. Machray profoundly disliked the provisional government of Louis Riel, but he refused to counsel any actions on the part of his people that might lead to violence. McLean, especially, was active in providing spiritual guidance for the prisoners being held by the provisional government at Upper Fort Garry, and he was instrumental in gaining the reprieve from execution of Captain Charles Arkoll Boulton. He was not able similarly to help Thomas Scott.

Over the summer of 1870 the province of Manitoba came into existence. On 3 May 1871 the college was incorporated by an act of the first legislature of Manitoba. Incorporation allowed the college to hold endowments. This action should not be confused with a charter. At the time the constitution of the college described its purposes as being to prepare fit persons for the sacred ministry, to provide instruction in the higher branches of education usually taught in universities, and to provide a collegiate school. These educational functions remained basic to the college for many years. In the spring of 1871 Warden McLean travelled across Canada and collected $8383.21 in financial support, including $435.25 he obtained while visiting the United States. The college council, which first met 31 July 1871, included by 1875 the bishop, McLean, Abraham Cowley, professors Grisdale and O'Meara, as well as Dr. Curtis Bird, MLA, the Honourable Colin Inkster, MLC, and Frederick Molyneux St. John, who had come to Manitoba with the Wolseley Expedition and was first clerk of the legislature and first secretary of the Protestant Board of Education. Since the religious makeup of the first Manitoba Legislative Assembly was twelve Catholics, eleven Anglicans, and one Presbyterian—and subsequent ones were not dissimilar—it is hardly surprising that the college council would consist of prominent Anglicans who were also among the political leaders of the new province.

Machray returned to England later in 1871, seeking a college endowment. In the course of his travels he frequently found it necessary to counter what he described as the common English view of Manitoba as a place of "nine months' snow and three months' mosquitoes." He put the funding case chiefly in terms of the need for clergymen to prevent the Church of England from losing its historic advantage and becoming overwhelmed by other Protestant denominations, as had already happened in Minnesota. His province would soon be filling up with a "coming multitude, this new nation of white men, mainly, doubtless of Anglo-Saxon blood—with all their struggles for this world, carrying with them the common human burden of sin with all its sorrows." Such arguments enabled Machray to collect a large sum of money, over £5000 up front, and commitments for another £130 per year. A number of donations to the college library were also made at this time—including ones from both Oxford and Cambridge university presses, as well as 400 volumes from John Macallum's widow— that more than doubled the number of its volumes. The Queen herself donated an autographed copy of her *Leaves from the Journal of Our Life in the Highlands.** The library donations suggest that the contributors had some broader vision for the college than merely a theological seminary. Few of these books survive in the college collection, however. The bishop would describe the college library to synod in 1873 as "excellent, especially for a Theological student." On his return to Canada Machray picked up another £8000 in Ontario and Quebec.

By early 1873 a report to the diocesan synod indicated that the college had three faculty members, all in the theological school, and the collegiate had a number of masters, some of them part-time. No evidence exists to suggest that there was at this time either a faculty teaching at the university

---

* This volume disappeared many years ago.

level or university-level courses being offered. There was an endowment producing £200 per annum for the professor of systematic divinity, and a general endowment of eighty pounds per year. The bill of fare in the curriculum was lean and limited, typical of its day. The courses taught in the college school for that year were mathematics, arithmetic, Latin, Greek, German, French, English literature, and music. No secular history was offered, although it must be added that the subject was not yet generally available in most institutions of higher learning. In 1875 the professorship of ecclesiastical history ("including the early Scriptures and the Book of Common Prayer") previously held by Machray was endowed. No courses in science were offered apart from mathematics, and none in moral philosophy. The theological school taught ecclesiastical history, systematic theology, Hebrew, and biblical literature. When Archdeacon McLean left to become bishop of Saskatchewan in 1873, Bishop Machray became warden of the college and headmaster of the collegiate, a combined position he continued to hold for many years. Machray also served as bursar in the early years, finally turning the duties over to the dean of the college in 1885. In 1874 Machray would move from Bishop's Court into rooms in the college building, eating most of his meals in the college dining room. Machray ate his evening meal precisely at nine o'clock, with the masters only. It consisted of cold meat and a single glass of beer. The bishop returned to the bishop's residence in the early 1880s.

An increasing number of denominational colleges were open in Manitoba by 1873, mainly in Winnipeg. St. Boniface College, first founded in 1818, had been incorporated along with St. John's College in 1871. It was modelled on the "college classique" of Quebec and was directed until 1878 by the Oblate Fathers. Manitoba College, founded in Kildonan in 1869 to serve the education needs of the Presbyterian community, came under the direction of the Reverend George Bryce. It would move to Winnipeg in 1874. A Wesleyan institute had also opened in 1873 on the corner of Main and Water streets in Winnipeg. It was not yet teaching at the university level, but soon hoped to be doing so. Many worried about the proliferation of these denominational schools. In 1872, when the Rev. George Grant had visited Winnipeg, he expressed typical Upper Canadian reformist concern that "the little Province with its fifteen thousand inhabitants will therefore soon rejoice in three or four denominational 'Colleges.'" The fear apparently was that the "mistakes" of Ontario and the Maritime provinces would be repeated in Manitoba. What precisely those "mistakes" consisted of was never entirely clear, although the notion that denominational education was an impediment to educational progress had early entered the mythology of the history of higher education in Canada.

Presumably the major concern about the proliferation of denominational colleges was that the duplication of facilities was unnecessarily expensive, and would prevent any single institution from being able to afford more than the basics, including the special facilities required for scientific and professional education. As Bishop Machray declared to his synod in 1875, "I should be as opposed as anyone to the creation of small denominational universities vainly competing with one another for the resources placed by the Province at the disposal of an undenominational university and by the unwholesome rivalry of petty interest lowering the standard of scholarship." This statement begged several questions, including the one about the size of the resources to be committed by the province to higher education. In Manitoba, for over a quarter of a century these resources would consist of a relative pittance, mainly the revenue from provincial marriage licences and later from the rental or sale of wasteland set aside as a university endowment. What Machray's statement in the context of 1875 meant was that he wished to disassociate himself and St. John's College from any movement toward denominational universities. Perhaps this reflected concerns from his synod delegates. In the meantime, each major denomination unquestionably needed its own training ground for an educated ministry, and no evidence has ever been presented that large institutions offered better basic secular educations to students than small ones, although obviously the curricula and the courses taught would be more limited. The chief concern of the non-denominationalists appears to have been to spend as little money on higher education as possible, which may or may not have been an approach to applaud.

As well, there were perceived social implications to denominational education. In 1876 the Reverend James Robertson—an Upper Canadian-born Presbyterian clergyman of Winnipeg's Knox Presbyterian Church, active in Manitoba College and subsequently superintendent of Presbyterian missionaries for Manitoba and the Northwest Territories from 1881 to 1902—would tell a Winnipeg audience at a meeting at Manitoba College that "denominational colleges were not so successful as those under the state." Sectarian colleges "made men narrow," he argued. At a state college the best men could mingle together and the "tendency would be to make the population homogeneous." Bishop Machray ought to have been able to see through these arguments, which once again came from the stable of Upper Canadian Clear Grit ideology and which were on the verge of entering Manitoba culture as Ontario exerted its intellectual and cultural domination in the province. Instead of rejecting such rationalizations, Bishop Machray bought into them. The process by which he got to supporting public secular education was a bit complicated.

By 1874, for Bishop Machray the principal goal to be achieved for St. John's College had become one of certification. More particularly, Machray wanted for the college a charter that would permit it to grant its graduates theological degrees. Why Machray constrained himself to theological degrees is partially revealed in a letter he subsequently wrote in 1875 to the Archbishop of Canterbury. He insisted that he opposed "the creation here of Denominational Universities as in the old Provinces of Canada, Church of England, Roman Catholic, Presbyterian, Wesleyan for granting Degrees in Arts, Medicine and Law. I purpose supporting a United University for Arts, etc., to which I should wish to affiliate St. John's College." Where Machray had gotten the Canadian educational information on which this statement is based is not at all clear, although the Reverend George Bryce and the Reverend James Roberston at Manitoba College are likely candidates as informants. Despite this statement, it appears unlikely that Machray was terribly interested in secular education at the university level. Unlike Bishop John Strachan a quarter-century earlier in Canada, Machray had no wish for Anglican control of general or professional education in the province of Manitoba. Instead, he conceded such education to the secular sphere and apparently decided to concentrate instead on the training of ministers and missionaries. For this he needed a degree-granting institution, but only for theological degrees. Thus he requested of the province's Lieutenant-Governor, Lord Dufferin, that an appropriate charter be sought from Canadian Prime Minister Alexander Mackenzie. As it turned out, the prime minister opposed chartering denominational schools. Mackenzie was a Clear Grit who believed in voluntary and non-sectarian education as an article of faith; such an attitude was one of the consequences of the behaviour of Machray's distinguished predecessor Archdeacon John Strachan of the Anglican Church of Upper Canada in the 1830s and 1840s in attempting to maintain an Anglican monopoly of higher education in the province. Mackenzie was also a cheese-paring Scot who would not spend a dollar if a dime would do the job. He told Dufferin that he understood that the Archbishop of Canterbury could provide the power for theological degrees.

St. John's College was obviously a thriving institution in a growing community in the early 1870s. Over the summer of 1874 the college building had been greatly enlarged with a large wing to its south to provide new classrooms, a library, a dining hall, rooms for masters and lecturers, bedrooms for the students, as well as a kitchen and servant quarters. The result was the white wooden building with a veranda across its front so familiar from old photographs. Sixty students were in residence, and the day students included the elder sons of the Lieutenant-Governor, who had earlier written the Governor General how pleased he was with their progress. There was also at water's edge a meteorological station, financed by the Dominion government since the summer of 1871, which sent back to Ottawa daily reports of weather conditions on the Red River; Charles Camsell has left us an account in the 1880s of tending this station. Most of the boarders were sons of Hudson's Bay Company officers. Boarding rates as of 1 August 1875 were set at seventy-five dollars per term for boys under sixteen, and eighty-five dollars per term for boys over sixteen. After that date, no boy under eight could be admitted to the school or as a boarder unless he had passed the "Second Reader," and all boarders over the age of fifteen had to be nominated by the Church Missionary Society. Further expansion included a small gymnasium and Divinity Hall, a two-storey building with a first-floor classroom and four upstairs bedrooms to accommodate student boarders. Still more bedrooms were installed over the college bakery and at Bishop's Court. Chapel services were held daily, but no dedicated building (or even room) existed for them. Success led to the formal creation of a body of alumni, including council members, honourary fellows, theological and other graduate members, and associates in arts. The alumni were expected to pay one dollar per year, half to go the library fund and half to the college fund. By 1876 Machray told synod that the present staff could teach twice the numbers if not required to instruct at higher levels, but the size of the school could not be expanded in its present buildings, and there were twelve boys awaiting Christmas admission.

One of the disadvantages of attending St. John's College was that it was able to offer no certification for its students—theological or otherwise—if they sought to go outside the province for further education or study. Bishop Machray on 17 April 1875 followed up on the advice from the prime minister, and wrote to the Archbishop of Canterbury requesting a charter for theological degrees "directly from the Queen." The archbishop replied that he could not help, for such matters were beyond his powers, but he submitted the question to the colonial secretary, Lord Carnarvon, who in turn wrote for information on charters from the Governor General.

The result was that the whole question was returned to Prime Minister Mackenzie, who promptly referred it to his Privy Council. That august body reported, in accordance with the Liberal Party line on the respective powers of Dominion and provincial legislatures, that granting an educational charter was a provincial, not a federal, matter. When this opinion was conveyed to Lord Carnarvon, that worthy (who obviously knew nothing about the Canadian constitution) told the Archbishop of Canterbury early in 1876 that it was his judgement that a province could not empower the granting of degrees that had to be recognized outside its jurisdiction, adding "it would be impossible for me to advise Her Majesty to confer the power of granting such degrees upon a Provincial College, such power being strictly reserved to the Great Universities in Great Britain and in the foreign dependencies of this country hereafter established in the Colonies." Exactly what Carnarvon was trying to convey here is not entirely clear. He was certainly wrong in his perception that provinces could not authorize the granting of universally recognized degrees—other provinces had already done so—and appears mainly to have been, in typical inflexible British imperial fashion, jealously preserving the right of the "great universities" of Britain to monopolize degrees. Thus the possibility of theological degrees from St. John's College seems to have been initially thwarted by the heady brew of Canadian Liberal Party provincial rights doctrine and British imperial establishment hostility to the colonies.

At about the same time that Machray's request for a theological college charter was being denied by the colonial secretary on totally specious grounds, the synod of Rupert's Land, at its annual meeting on 12 January 1876, passed an enactment declaring that "until Degrees can be obtained by the alumni of the College, the Council may by examination or otherwise, confer the titles of Associate in Arts, and Associate in Divinity." This motion suggests that the synod was not concerned only with theological degrees. As Laurie Wilmot, a later warden of the college, has pointed out in his unpublished thesis on the origins of the University of Manitoba, this synod's immediate predecessor had among its delegates the Honourable Colin Inkster (a member of the legislative council of the province), the Honourable John Norquay, minister of public works in the Manitoba government and later premier of the province, and Chief Justice Edmund Wood, all of whom were also members of the St. John's College council. The question of a degree-granting institution for the province of Manitoba was obviously an issue of some concern, at least to some of its political leaders.

Within a few weeks of the Rupert's Land synod's vote, a number of speakers at a prize-giving convocation at Manitoba College discussed the question of a university and the possible models for its organization. American consul James Wickes Taylor suggested affiliating the several denominational colleges of the province under a single board of regents, as had been done in New York state. Nobody in the province would ever seriously follow up on the New York model, since a more familiar and congenial University of London model of colleges grouped around a fictional degree-granting authority was also available. Prof. George Bryce added his hope that the government would organize a common board for higher education, with some scholarships and a common examination. Prof. Thomas Hart of Wesley College concurred with Bryce and advocated the swift creation of a provincial university. As for the major speaker, the Reverend James Robertson, he noted that there were "a large number of students in the denominational collegiate institutes, and some of these want to prosecute their studies further." He did not suggest that there were any university-level students already in the system. In this statement Robertson may well have been misinformed about the situation at St. John's College, but the weight of the evidence suggests that he was quite right. St. John's had no more university-level students than any other institution because it was not teaching at the university level.

Not long after the Manitoba College convocation, Bishop Machray wrote on 28 February 1876 to Lieutenant-Governor Alexander Morris, rehearsing his problems in obtaining a charter for St. John's College that would permit the institution to grant theological degrees. Machray knew perfectly well that Morris had two sons who would be ready to go to university in 1877, and therefore—even though his sons would be heading back east—understood the urgency of the problem. He concluded by threatening, if further thwarted on the theological degree front, to affiliate St. John's College to an English university. This would affect all degrees, not merely those in divinity, he noted, adding, "I am not anxious to build up a Denominational University—

on the contrary I am prepared to give my whole influence to the building up of an Undenominational University in Arts, Law, Medicine, and Science." The bishop went even further at this point, proposing a provincial university with "a common faculty for Degrees in Arts, Law, Medicine, Science, and separate Faculties belonging to the individual Colleges for Theology." This, it should be noted, was the sort of system of higher education that Machray wanted, rather than the one he ultimately got in 1877.

Because so much confusion has persisted over the situation of St. John's College in these early years, it is certainly worth summing it up as of 1877, on the eve of the formal establishment of the University of Manitoba. Bishop Machray had re-established St. John's College in 1866. Whether the re-establishment constituted a fresh founding is an open question. In any event, although Machray recognized and spoke of three functions for the college—theological training, pre-university-level education, and university-level work of a secular nature—he had up to 1877 dealt only with the first two functions. A theological college existed, as did a collegiate school. Machray had not introduced secular education at the university level into St. John's College, partly because his model for St. John's College was not particularly the Oxbridge college one, partly because he hoped that secular education would be taken up by a provincial university when it was organized in the near future. Machray was on the other side of the nineteenth-century debate over the role of religion in higher education. He had conceded that secular education at the university level was the role of the state, and he therefore wanted as little to do with it as possible. The church should be able to conserve its resources, financial and otherwise, for the tasks that ought to be within its mandate, and not worry about matters beyond its concern. Subsequent events beyond his control would force Machray into conceding that St. John's College would have to engage in university-level secular education, as we shall see, but he never favoured such activity. The result would be that St. John's College had to undergo yet another transformation.

Chapter Three

Adding Liberal Arts, 1877–1892

WINNIPEG AND THE ENTIRE CANADIAN WEST BEGAN TO BOOM in the late 1870s with the arrival of the railroad. The establishment of the University of Manitoba in 1877 was symptomatic of the spirit of confidence being felt about the future. The boom really took off in Winnipeg in 1881 and lasted until 1883, when the inevitable bust set in. The city began to think of itself as "the Chicago of the North," the economic hub of the entire prairie region. Immigrants from outside the British Empire began to move into the north end of Winnipeg, surrounding the Anglican enclave of the cathedral and the college on the banks of the Red River with the crowded tenements housing the newcomers, most of whom lived in poverty. Everywhere the Anglican Church was challenged to serve the expanding population of the city, province, and region, at the same time that it discovered only a relatively small proportion of the recent arrivals were likely to become parishioners or communicants. The church tried to embrace the expansion rather than to respond by feeling beleaguered.

Winnipeg in this period was part of "a mighty empire." Its polyglot population was dominated by people of British stock from Ontario and the British Isles, who comprised the city's middle and upper classes. The "foreign element" made up the rest of the population. The elite consisted of no more than 400 people, the number of invitations issued to the annual Cricket Club Ball. The guest list was published and consisted of almost exclusively Anglo names. The English controlled the civil service, the Scots the police force, the Irish the fire department. The non-Anglos were relegated to low-status jobs in construction and in the railway shops. The Anglican, Presbyterian, and Methodist churches were the leading religious bodies. Fraternal organizations like the Sons of Englishmen (with five local lodges), the St. Andrew's Society, and the Orange Order were extremely prominent. The Sons of Englishmen lodges were led by Anglican clergy, many of them associated with St. John's College, the educational establishment of the English in Winnipeg—at least in the popular mind—as much as the St. Boniface College was that of the francophone population, Manitoba College that of the Presbyterian Scots and Irish, and Wesley College of the Methodists.

Bishop Robert Machray would no doubt have been most unpleasantly surprised to learn that later chroniclers of both St. John's College and the University of Manitoba have tended to treat his involvement in the founding of the university as something of a personal triumph. In truth, the university as created in 1877 was a considerable setback for Machray, who had hoped to push off all university-level secular teaching to the new institution. Instead, the way in which the University of Manitoba was organized in 1877 forced St. John's College to open what amounted to its own faculty of arts and sciences, in order to share fully in the burden of teaching now imposed on it by the enabling legislation.

As chairman of the Manitoba Board of Education, Bishop Machray had met frequently over the years with those of his fellows in the province involved in the colleges. He had many discussions with them about the introduction of a non-sectarian system of higher education; certainly Machray's colleagues among the Presbyterians and Methodists were in full agreement with the concept of publicly funded university. There were two problems, however. One was that the province felt that it had little or no money to contribute to the scheme. The other was that Bishop Alexandre-Antonin Taché, the Roman Catholic leader of the province, had grave objections to surrendering the autonomy of St. Boniface College to a public institution. Taché was willing to allow, however, that the model of the University of London offered a solution to his objections, and early in 1877 his college agreed to join in the creation of a university in Manitoba, providing that all rights, obligations, and privileges of the college would be maintained, and that the college would continue to have absolute control over its teaching and administration.

The result of the St. Boniface conditions and the provincial lack of money was that the University of Manitoba, as brought into existence, was a quite different creature from the one envisioned by Bishop Machray in 1876. Machray, it will be recalled, had wanted a non-denominational public university in arts, law, medicine, and science, with separate faculties belonging to the individual colleges for theology. What he got instead was a federated university consisting of autonomous denominational colleges, in which the university functions consisted of nothing more than examining candidates for degrees and the granting of these degrees. This arrangement (the University of London model) was the least expensive of all possible options from the government's standpoint, throwing almost all the expenses of higher education (including the costs of cooperation) back to the colleges. The first annual grant from the province would be for the munificent sum of $250! The *Free Press* was certainly supportive of any scheme that would not "be a heavy burden upon the finances of the Province," and Attorney General Joseph Royal, in introducing the enabling legislation for the university on behalf of the government, emphasized that the colleges would bear virtually all the costs.

The legislation was amended in committee of the whole by inserting the phrase "at present" in subsection 5 after the phrase "there shall be no Professorship or other teachership in the University," and by omitting the specific reference to the University of London as model. These changes were not well publicized at the time, however, for as Bishop Machray pointed out in his subsequent history of the university, he did not know of them and had certainly objected to the original version of the bill for failing to provide for the eventual establishment of a teaching body. Machray was not a whiner, however. At the diocesan synod of May 1877, he declared his approval of the passage of the bill, which was, he said, "about as satisfactory as could be devised in the immediate condition of things." He added that the bill gave the denominations the power of "establishing in their Colleges a Faculty for conferring theological degrees." What he did not observe was that the legislation also meant that St. John's College had some responsibility for secular undergraduate teaching, an area in which it had not previously been active. Machray may well have taken on the chancellorship of the new university to help him in making the adjustments that would be necessary at the college. The bishop obviously felt that the price of gaining theological degrees was one worth paying, although it would involve St. John's College in additional expenditures.

Machray acted without delay at the 23 May 1877 meeting of synod to get the authorization for the formation of a theological faculty. The college council, less than a month later (19 June 1877), duly voted to create a faculty of divinity. That faculty would consist of the professors of ecclesiastical history, systematic theology, and exegetical theology. Examiners for these departments, as well as for Hebrew, Greek, and Latin, were also added. The council then elected a number of honourary fellows, including former bishop Anderson, Alexander K. Isbister, and Adam Thom, as well as seven members to represent the college on the senate of the newly created university. The new senators were A. Cowley, Canon Grisdale, Canon O'Meara, Rev. N. Young, Rev. O. Fortin, Rev. S.P. Matheson, and John Norquay (who would soon become premier of the province). At a council meeting in August

1877, an address to Governor General Lord Dufferin—who was planning to visit the college—was agreed upon. It briefly rehearsed the history of the college, and emphasized, "hitherto the College has had a Grammar School for Higher Education and a Theological School for Students in Theology." The address continued: "a further effort must soon be undertaken by us. Your Excellency is probably aware that an Act was passed last Session by the Legislature of Manitoba founding a University. St. John's College is one of the Colleges of this University, taking part in its Government and hoping to have the privilege of preparing Students for its course of Studies & Degree Examinations. This will soon require a separate Building and an increased staff of Teachers." The address was circumspect enough not to ask directly for money, but the need was certainly well expressed.

The three newly affiliated colleges—St. John's, St. Boniface, and Manitoba—had to work out a common academic structure and curriculum for non-theological education. This was less difficult than might have been otherwise imagined, or has been suggested by earlier historians of the college, because none of the institutions involved had any serious record or history of secular undergraduate education. They may have inherited models, but not actual practices, and so they were working out a new structure as they went along. Only Manitoba College actually had a handful of non-theological university students already enrolled. Representatives of the colleges met together to agree upon a curriculum of studies and examination procedures. They decided to follow the practice of English colleges of awarding a Bachelor of Arts degree—in the following subjects: classics, mathematics, natural science, and modern languages (German, French, and English). They also determined to observe the English practice of written examinations, and followed the pattern at Cambridge colleges, not surprising, given Machray's presence as chairman of these meetings. Students could take either an "ordinary" or an "honours" degree.

The "Preliminary" examination was written at the outset to determine whether the candidate was fit for higher education. The second examination, the "Previous," was written at the end of the first year to decide whether the student could proceed to the BA in two years of study in one of a number of modules of courses: special or honours classics, mathematics, natural science, moral and mental philosophy, modern languages, and a general program. Another examination was written at the end of the second year, the Junior BA examination. At the close of the third year, the Senior BA examination was held, used to divide students into three classes according to merit. According to the University Act, students could write in either French or English. This system was subsequently adopted for the theological school in April 1880, when the requirements for the papers were set forth in considerable detail. This, of course, was the "tripos" transported to North America for a few years, at least.

According to Bishop Machray's biographer, his nephew Robert Machray, some time in early October 1877 the bishop sent him and five other students to the residence of the newly appointed registrar of the university to become matriculated. Four of the students were theological students, and the other two were the head boys of the college school. There were no arts students because there was as yet no arts program actually in place. The six walked to the registrar's home in Point Douglas and a spokesman indicated their errand. The registrar "smiled and looked a little blank, observing that there was no University Register yet in existence. However, he was equal to the occasion, produced a half-sheet of ordinary writing-paper, and bade them inscribe their names upon it!" In September 1878 the University of Manitoba council agreed to admit seven students who had passed necessary examinations. W.R. Gunn had passed the Previous, and the other six the Preliminary. All seven were students at Manitoba College.

Gradually the system settled in. Matriculation, or entrance examination, came after a Preliminary examination, which could be attempted by anyone in the province. Students needed 25 percent in every subject to pass the Preliminary examination, and 66.6 percent in all subjects constituted a "first." The Preliminary examination was designed to weed out the unprepared, and the preparation involved classical subjects. After the first year, students sat the Previous examination before proceeding to special honours or general courses. Subjects for the Previous examination were Latin, Greek, modern languages (including English), and mathematics, for a total of thirteen separate papers. The same percentages as for Preliminary examinations applied. Special or honours courses required specialization in a subject with high academic standing. In both courses, students wrote an examination after the second year, known as the Junior examination, and after the third year wrote the Senior or Final examination. These upper-level examinations required 34 percent in each paper and a 40 percent average, with higher grades in some subjects. The emphasis in the examination results was on standing (first, second, third, pass), which was usually published in the local newspapers. Actual percentages were published after 1896.

Examination results were a matter of considerable competition among the colleges in the early days, and the number of firsts and medal winners collected by a college was a mark of its standing in the community. In May 1893, for example, of eighty-four medals, forty-eight went to Manitoba College, nineteen to St. John's College, fourteen to St. Boniface College, and three to Wesley College. The number of medallists was more or less commensurate with the number of graduands. Up to 1894, 148 students graduated from Manitoba College, seventy from St. John's College, twenty-one from St. Boniface College, and twenty-eight from Wesley College. Of these graduands, thirty-five from Manitoba received honours degrees in natural science (24 percent, including five Governor General's silver medallists), ten from St. John's (14 percent) had honours degrees in natural science, none from St. Boniface College had honours degrees in natural science, and two (7 percent) from Wesley held natural science honours degrees. Three Johnians, two Wesley people, two Manitoba people, and no St. Boniface people received degrees in mathematics.

The university component of St. John's College teaching was chiefly the traditional classical one developed in both Britain and France, emphasizing ancient languages and mathematics and designed chiefly to prepare students for holy orders. Textbooks were carefully prescribed. Teaching was done in the colleges by individuals who carried heavy loads, often up to forty hours in the classroom a week. They had little incentive for research. Many of the early teachers were long remembered as hard-working and harried men. Instruction emphasized rote memorization and recitation. Material learned had to be retained long enough for the end-of-year examinations administered by the university but prepared by the teachers in the colleges. For neither faculty nor students was there a clear division between the theological part of the college and the secular academic part. Most Johnians prepared for examinations in arts and theology simultaneously, and the divinity professors taught all the courses in all three years of the arts program. Enrolment grew slowly. St. John's students wrote seven papers beyond the preliminary level in 1879, and six in 1880. The teaching staff in 1882 had reached seventeen; all but one of them—the lecturer in music—were Church of England clergymen. The number of undergraduates proceeding to the bachelor of divinity were three, and the number of undergraduates proceeding to either the BA or BD totalled seventeen.

Following the establishment of the university, Bishop Machray doubled his efforts to raise funds for his college, fully conscious that he had to accommodate arts undergraduates as well as theological students and those in the collegiate school. He was also aware that the population of Manitoba was growing rapidly, that homestead land was being taken up in increasing amounts, and that a railroad was on the verge of reaching Winnipeg. Moreover, eastern Canadian Protestant denominations—chiefly the Methodists and Presbyterians—were sending well-financed missionaries into the West in large numbers, while the Church of England got little assistance, financial or otherwise, from eastern Canada. On his visit to England in 1878–79 to attend the second Lambeth Conference, Machray made a number of desperate appeals for funding. Britain was in the midst of a severe depression, which hampered the campaign. But the Society for the Propagation of Christian Knowledge voted £500 for the endowment of each of the chairs of exegetical theology and ecclesiastical history, £1000 for a college building fund, and £380 for three years for scholarships. The Society for the Propagation of the Gospel devoted most of its small amount of available funds to Rupert's Land.

The economic buoyancy of the Manitoba economy at the end of the 1870s and the beginning of the 1880s had some implications for the college as well. A sense of optimism prevailed about the future. As early as October 1876 the college council discussed the organization of a "Ladies School" for "the daughters of the upper classes in the Province of Rupert's Land." It agreed to establish such a school, to be called the "St. John's College Ladies School." The bishop's inclination was to promote a boarding school for females adjacent to the college school, utilizing school staff, but he feared that such a school would not be patronized by families in the city; only four day boys from Winnipeg attended the collegiate school in 1875. Nothing further was done in this matter until 1879, when college council heard notice of the incorporation of "St. John's College Ladies School." The school was to be governed by a board consisting of the bishop as president, and Rev. Henry Wright, honourary secretary of the Church Missionary Society, as vice-president, plus twelve other members. At the request of the college council and the board of governors of the ladies' school, synod accepted the trust of the property. According to Bishop Machray's report to the diocesan synod in late 1880, a building for the ladies' school had been erected free of debt, chiefly because a private donor gave £2000 for the purpose. The building was on a three-acre lot near the cathedral between the river and Main Street. Nevertheless, the school was not yet a paying proposition, and was already $5000 in debt. On 19 December 1881, a deed conveyed land to the St. John's College Ladies School—part of lot 40—from St. John's College.

A personal visit and appeal for funds in eastern Canada in 1881 by Bishop Machray—calling on Ontario Anglicans to match the efforts of the Presbyterians and Methodists—raised a paltry $860. A subsequent fundraising effort in England focussing on the arts side of the college and led by Canon Grisdale (who was by 1882 Dean of Rupert's Land) was an almost total bust. Grisdale carried a circular prepared by the bishop that pointed out the desperate need for trained men in the West. Fortunately, Machray was able to capitalize on the Winnipeg land boom of the early 1880s, selling substantial amounts of cathedral land at inflated prices and gaining subscriptions from local businessmen of $20,000 for the college building fund. The sale of the cathedral land seemed to make possible a proper endowment for the cathedral, and by late 1881 Machray could tell the provincial synod that about half of the cost of a new wing for the college had been raised. Somehow or other, the new wing would become a new building.

Planning and construction of the new college building began in 1882, when the boom allowed visions of grandeur to soar. An architect's drawing of 1883 shows a greatly expanded college complex consisting of a series of interconnected buildings, its spires clearly suggesting a Cambridge college model. Only a small section of this grandiose structure was ever built. Contemporaries referred to it as the "first wing," but it was indeed the only part of the plan ever completed. It was located on a four-acre lot on the west side of Main Street at Church Avenue, two blocks from the river and from the college school and cathedral. The new building was a three-and-a-half-storey brick structure (partially constructed with bricks from a nearby brickyard that rented land from the college and paid some of its rent in bricks) with a tower (not a spire!) on either end. It had considerable classroom space and provided residential accommodation for twenty students. It was also very expensive to construct, particularly given the interior heating and plumbing that was installed, and Bishop Machray told the synod in 1884 that the construction debt stood at $55,000. Additional expenditures had also been made on a house for the deputy headmaster, facilities for the matron and a hospital, and a double brick house for two masters. Worse still, $12,000 of the subscriptions promised for the building fund had not come in or had been paid in land that could not be sold and turned into cash. The ladies' school had proved equally expensive. The fees were only half of those of comparable institutions in the United States and Canada, and could not be raised if students were to be attracted. The board of governors tried to close down the ladies' school that year, but the wife of Deacon Cowley took over the financial responsibility, and the school remained open. It still had a substantial debt for which the college was responsible. That debt reached $12,000 by 1885.

Despite the expenses, Machray and his diocese soldiered on. As has been pointed out by William Fraser, who wrote the centennial history of St. John's College, the record of the Church of England in creating competing institutions of higher learning in western Canada was not very prepossessing. Bishop McLean had tried to establish a college in Saskatchewan in 1879, but shortly after his death in 1886 it was converted into a residential boarding school for Aboriginal children. A college in Qu'Appelle opened in 1885 but closed its doors a few years later. Bishop Machray had good reason for believing that St. John's College would have to bear the burden of theological training on the Prairies for a good many years to come.

The years of the boom were in many ways misleading. Reports of the economic state of Winnipeg in the early 1880s persuaded many in eastern Canada that the Diocese of Rupert's Land was in splendid shape financially, having benefited greatly from the sale of its land. One eastern bishop had written to Bishop Machray in 1882 of information he had received that the Manitoba Church was "bloated with money from the Boom." As it turned out, the cathedral lands had been sold mainly on credit. Over the years most of the property reverted to the cathedral after foreclosures, meaning that the bulk of the so-called endowment had been lost. At the same time, the church and college in Manitoba had clearly overexpanded on buildings, and they would have to pay the price. People in eastern Canada and in England were still persuaded that, as one newspaper article in the *English Guardian* claimed in June 1885, the Diocese of Rupert's Land was "the richest and best-endowed Diocese in Canada." Moreover, this writer insisted that the diocese had spent money on education and a splendid cathedral that it should have been spending on missions.

Machray was forced to defend himself in print, and the synod appointed a committee to investigate the financial state of St. John's College, which reported to the diocesan synod in August 1886. The report revealed no financial improprieties, but made clear that maintaining the college was an expensive proposition to which the government contributed little. The college in 1885 had received $1568.25 from the province as its share of the marriage licence fund, and the whole sum received since 1879, covering seven and one-half years, totalled only $3514.93. The college appreciated that it could not afford to fund a university, but it could certainly be more munificent in aid to the province's colleges. In his earlier written defence, Machray insisted that "the Cathedral and College system of St. John's have been the salvation of the country," but not every member of the diocese would necessarily have concurred. The cathedral and the college shared an endowment of $131,856, and the college had a general endowment fund of $22,000 and a scholarship fund of $6695. The college debt, incurred in erecting buildings, stood at $60,000.

The August 1886 report included a list of the numbers of students who attended the college from 1866 to 1885, and noted "it is only since 1882 that a separation has been made between the boys attending the school and the students attending the college."

YEAR	BOYS	YEAR	BOYS	YEAR	BOYS	STUDENTS
1866	29	1873	47	1880	78	
1867	36	1874	69	1881	87	
1868	42	1875	74	1882	81	13
1869	36	1876	75	1883	71	17
1870	28	1877	68	1884	76	14
1871	28	1878	69	1885	70	15
1872	29	1879	80	1886	69	21

In 1886 five professors and three masters were employed in full-time teaching. The numbers of students at St. John's College, the report added, was quite comparable to those at other Anglican colleges; Lennoxville, Quebec, for example, had twenty-one students and sixty-two boys, plus four professors and five masters.

The report also documented the substantial amounts of money the bishop had given to the college, especially to endow professorships and for the ladies' college. As well, this report demonstrated the multiplicity of courses taught to small numbers in the BA program, which had twenty students in total. In the junior BA year, for example, there were two students in classical honours, one in mathematics honours, one in mental and moral science honours, one in modern language honours, and one in natural science honours. Moreover, the number of students taught could be substantially increased without much addition to the staff, except that broadening the list of subjects taught always required new appointments, and the university was very good at constant expansion of the curriculum.

The staff worked hard. Andrew Baird at Manitoba College later recalled that professors at his institution taught daily from 9 a.m. to 3 p.m. with an hour to eat at midday, and the school day at St. John's was similar. Some of the theological school professors at St. John's College were decently paid out of the substantial cathedral endowment; each canon professor was paid $1700 per year, for example. This was not an excessive salary in an age in which an unskilled labourer earned less than two dollars a day. But by comparison with parish clergy, who earned about $700 a year, it may have seemed very generous and may have contributed to a growing gulf between clergy teaching at the college and those ministering in the parishes. At the same time, the increasing demands of secular university instruction pressed heavily on St. John's, being met with the appointments of temporary and/or part-time instructors, usually local parish clergymen.

In 1887 the appointment of Edgar Kenrick (a University of Toronto graduate and a layman) as a lecturer in natural science provided additional dimensions to the problem. The distance of Manitoba College from St. John's College had made it difficult for the two institutions to cooperate in science, and Kenrick would require a laboratory, at least for demonstration purposes, in his teaching of chemistry, yet another expense.

An unexpected visitor arrived at the college in October 1886, and his diary offers us some picture of how it appeared to the outsider. The Reverend Daniel Greatorex of London was on a tour of Canada and stopped in Winnipeg to visit with Prof. O'Meara and his family for a few days. He called the college structure "a handsome brick building" and because his hosts ate with the students, he described the meal routine in some detail. Breakfast at 8:15 consisted of "Porridge, Meat, Bread & Butter & Tea." Dinner at 12:30 meant "Meat Vegetables and pudding"; no malt liquor or spirits were allowed in the building. Tea at 5:30 was "Tea, Bread & Butter and Jam." The college was clearly on a British dining regimen involving a substantial breakfast, the main meal at noon, and tea in the late afternoon. Greatorex was sufficiently impressed with the college to donate to it a few years later his collection of rare religious books. One of those books, a King James Bible, has recently been identified as a very valuable first edition.

The bishop made another fundraising trip to England after the 1886 synod report, but it raised less than £1500 for the college endowment. This discouraging result may have contributed to the sentiments the bishop imparted to the 1887 diocesan synod: he regarded the model of the University of London as unfortunate, he said, since it meant that a number of colleges were standing in for a university. He thought that for the immediate future the colleges should remain in charge of classics and mathematics, but that the university should teach the sciences and modern languages. He had always accepted that

> at some time in the future such professorships in the University would be established, and I have worked for St. John's College with the hope buoying me up that we had not before us what I should regard as the hopeless task of building up a college supplying the requirements as regards instruction of a great university of the present day, but simply a home in that university in which the sons of our church people, and any other students coming to us may, amid their secular studies and recreation, meet together daily as a family for morning and evening prayer.

As Bishop Machray well knew, the classical curriculum of the colleges was hardly designed to satisfy the pretensions of an up-and-coming young province. Almost from the creation of the university, therefore, pressure existed for the establishment of professional schools, the teaching of scientific and technical subjects, and a more practical vocationally oriented course of study. Against the wishes of the Manitoba College of Physicians and

Surgeons, a private medical school was organized in 1882 and affiliated with the university in 1883. This affiliation made it impossible for the university to continue solely as an examining and degree-granting body. A year later a reading course in law, providing three annual examinations leading to an LLB degree, was similarly accepted. Nevertheless, in 1885, when a land grant from the federal and provincial governments provided the first public financial support to the university beyond the marriage licence fees, the chancellor could still describe his institution as "a Republic of Colleges to which in conjunction with the Graduates of the University the State has practically committed the direction and government of the university." The land grant, provided for by acts of both the Dominion Parliament and the provincial legislature, was really a federal grant of Crown lands. It provided for 150,000 acres of land of "fair average quality" to be allowed to the university. Getting the lands and managing their disposal would be a slow business, and the land grant did not immediately provide any revenue for the university.

In 1885 a new window was opened into the life of St. John's College with the publication of the first issue of the *St. John's College Magazine.* This publication, which was sponsored by the college literary society and initially edited by Canon Coombes, a member of faculty, in conjunction with a number of students, came and went over a period of more than forty years. Originally intended to appear eight times a year, the magazine arrived the same year as a similar publication called *The Manitoba College Journal,* and thus was one of the first student publications in Canada west of southern Ontario. Not all issues have survived, and publishing interruptions—usually following a series of dire editorial warnings of the result of failure of subscribers to pay their subscriptions—were frequent. But enough early issues still exist to give a fairly complete picture of life in the college during its heyday before the appearance of competition from arts and sciences at the University of Manitoba. Not surprisingly, the recurrent complaint was the "lack of corporate life . . . amongst the students of the University of Manitoba."

In 1888 an association of alumni was organized at the annual Old Boys' Dinner, an event that had been taking place for several years. The dinner was an opportunity for those who attended the various incarnations of St. John's College, including Macallum's Academy and Bishop Anderson's school, to get together. In 1887 the oldest "Old Boy" present was the Reverend Thomas Cook of Westbourne, who had attended St. John's School in 1842. At the dinner in 1888 it was resolved that the association be named the "St. John's Alumni and Old Boys' Association," open to professors, masters, graduates, and former pupils of St. John's College in its various versions. That same year the University of Manitoba's "republic of colleges" was increased by the establishment of a Methodist theological college in Winnipeg called Wesley College.

A year later, in 1889, special meetings of the university council debated the question of the introduction of teaching by the university, and ended by a vote of nineteen to sixteen to establish a committee on the subject. That committee reported late in 1889, calling for the creation of at least five chairs in natural science, mathematics, and modern languages. The assumption was that the chairs would be funded out of the sale of university lands, but the federal government, under pressure from Bishop Taché, insisted that the conveyance of title to these lands state that they would be resumed by the government should the university change its present form of incorporation. This deadlock would not be broken until 1897. For many years the only income from the land grants was a small revenue from cutting wood and hay on the properties. In the meantime, the three Protestant colleges (St. John's, Manitoba, and Wesley) pooled their resources for the teaching of science. Edgar Kenrick was joined by George Bryce and George Laird as a science department operating out of rented rooms on the top floor of the McIntyre Block, a commercial building on Portage Avenue near Main Street. The space included two lecture rooms, a library, and laboratories in physics and chemistry, and was destroyed by fire in 1898. After the fire, science teaching moved to the Davis Block, opposite City Hall. By 1893 a committee of the university council was appointed to consider available sites for a university building in Winnipeg. The province refused to provide any funding until 1897, when it agreed to lend the university the sum of $60,000 to build and equip a science building, in return for a mortgage on the endowment lands. The government also agreed to an annual grant of $6000 for teaching, with $5000 more to be charged against the lands.

The college in the early 1890s also sponsored a number of ceremonial and public events over the course of the school year. Extra tramcars could be ordered from the street railway company if large crowds were expected. Such events included the annual commemoration in late October, at which school prizes were awarded. The "Commem" in 1891 concluded with a "Laughable Farce" performed by male students (some of whom took female parts). A student-faculty dinner was held not long after the Commemoration. The St. John's Choral Society offered an annual concert; the one in 1891 featured John Farmer's sacred oratorio "Christ and His Soldiers." The St. John's Lawn Tennis Club offered another concert in mid-November at the cathedral schoolhouse, which in 1891 offered the larghetto from Beethoven's *Second Symphony* performed by piano and strings and concluded with a string quartet.

In 1892 the first women students were admitted to St. John's College. This shift to coeducational status produced a fourth incarnation for the college, one that would last until 1922.

Chapter Four

A Coeducational College, 1892–1910

WINDS OF CHANGE BLEW OVER THE PRAIRIES in the late 1880s and 1890s. One of the main currents was the emergence of a new status for women, who in this period ceased to be the property of their husbands and became instead independent legal entities. Women began to agitate for political rights and to organize movements of social reform, particularly in the still expanding city of Winnipeg. Reform—of public health, of overindulgence in alcoholic beverages, of prostitution, of political corruption—became the watchword of the day among the middle classes. The province's farm communities came increasingly to view Winnipeg as Sodom and Gomorrah, and sought to insulate their children from the evils of the city. St. John's College shared in the new currents. It admitted women to undergraduate education in 1892, and in the new century found itself caught up in the protracted political battle over higher education in the province. The struggle over higher education involved many issues, but a major one centred on an effort both to protect the sons and daughters of farmers from the terrible city and to provide them with a practical education that would fit them to return to their agricultural communities as leaders. Other questions concerned the increasing secularism of modern society and the place of science in the new order.

Even after the appearance of the first women in the college in 1892, the ambiance of the place continued to be very much male-dominated. The ethos was that of the English public school or university—a sort of honourable and somewhat juvenile masculinity came to involve the development of character and the playing of the game—although it must be remembered as far as the juvenile nature was concerned that the college school was regarded by its administrators as the most important part of the institution. Charles Camsell, who enrolled in St. John's College School in 1884, would later describe its life at the time, at least in the old building, as "pretty rugged." Boarders were returned temporarily from the new building to the old building in that year as an economy measure.

In the winter, there was no central heating. The classrooms on the first floor were heated by woodstoves that were not fed at night. On the upper storeys there were a few coal-burning stoves in the main halls, but none anywhere near the rooms of the students. There was no plumbing, running water, or electricity. Water froze in the morning in the jugs and basins used for washing up. His fellow students, Camsell added, were "a primitive lot of young rascals many of whom had not acquired any habits of self discipline and undoubtedly gave the authorities a great deal of trouble." In a reminiscence published in the college magazine in 1912, the archbishop's nephew Robert Machray substantiated Camsell's account, adding that on cold winter mornings the boarders thrust red-hot pokers heated in the coal stoves into the icy water in the basins in order to break the ice.

Women were considerably disadvantaged in at least three senses in the period before 1910. First, they could not live in the residence of the college. Secondly, they could not participate on the college sports teams. And finally, they could not look forward to ordination, and thus were not able to be "theologues," the college students always preferred by the administration. On the other hand, because women could not be ordained, they were unlikely to study arts and theology simultaneously, and females constituted a substantial proportion of the arts and sciences student body of the years between 1892 and 1910.

Robert Machray observed in 1912 that in these early days, "the College and the School were inextricably mixed." It was "not till after the University was established that much of a distinction was made between them." A secret society called "Protatin," modelled on Greek letter societies, flourished among the boys, meeting in the library "at a late hour when the warden slumbered peacefully." It engaged in what one of its members called "harmless ritual." Starting fires in the old building was not uncommon and at least two major ones were caused by arson that occurred in this period. A good deal of prank-playing also occurred. Some of the pranks could be malicious, and generally targeted teachers not respected by the students. On one occasion, four senior students hid Mr. Kenrick's bicycle, damaging it in the process. When the machine was repaired, the students repeated their offence. The culprits were caught, threatened with expulsion, and forced both to pay the costs of repair and to write an apology to the victim.

Discipline was much harsher for boys under sixteen, most of the population of the collegiate school. They were subject to flogging by Bishop Machray himself, who meted out such punishments in ritual form once a week in his rooms, using a Scottish instrument called the tawse, "a leather strap cut in strips and knotted." Those thus punished universally testified that they had deserved it and were better for it. Residential life had other problems as well, including periodic outbreaks of contagious diseases. A scarlet fever epidemic in the college in 1893, for example, forced the closure of the residence and ultimately the entire operation of the school, costing the college a term's income.

In 1890, partly in another economical move and partly because of the obvious deficiencies in the "old building," the entire boarding population of the college and school had been moved to the new building. More than fifty-five boarders crowded into a space originally designed for twenty. The facilities remained in use as such for twenty-two years, and not until 1900 were "modern conveniences" installed in the building. The old building was subsequently abandoned. The ethos, especially among the older boys, included a good bit of pipe-smoking, a bit of hazing, the custom of "fagging" (younger boys acting as gofers for their elders), and a lot of active sports. This and a series of residency regulations taken from Westminster School in England were virtually all that St. John's inherited from its British roots, apart from the fascinating set of architectural drawings already mentioned that showed a proposed new college building looking very much like a Cambridge college. Although many authorities refer to the English colleges as models for St. John's College, certainly St. John's did not attempt after 1900 to replicate either the Cambridge tripos or, in detailed practice, the Oxbridge system of seminars and tutorials.

Perhaps not surprisingly, the first public debate recorded in the college magazine, held in November 1891, was focussed on the resolution "that the mental capacities of the female sex are equal to those of the male." Soon after the appearance of the first woman a year later, the college magazine announced the formation of "The St. John's Ladies' Students Aid Society," devoted to assisting students "in the needle-and-thread department," especially in the repair of sundry gowns. The female students were particularly active in the literary and dramatic societies, where their achievements could be properly appreciated. From its foundation in 1884 the St. John's College Choral Society featured many young women from the ladies' school. Women were often involved in the St. John's College Literary Society, especially at the frequent society evenings that turned into performance free-for-alls. Women were also part of the St. John's Operatic Society, which debuted on 11 and 12 December 1903 with a performance of Housley's operetta, *Love and Whist.*

The intellectual atmosphere in the college was not in general very highly elevated. One of the continual complaints of the college magazine in these years was the difficulty of gaining access to the college library, a two-storey room in the college building. It was open only a few minutes every week, the key was almost impossible to find—the college authorities would not distribute keys to students—and the books were badly shelved, making it almost impossible to locate anything. An additional problem was an absence of a cataloguing system, leading the magazine to observe that "hundreds of valuable books have become assimilated into the libraries of men from Halifax to Dawson City." Furthermore, the library was not properly heated.

A number of substantial donations were made over the years to the library. Former student Alexander K. Isbister (Red River Academy, 1833–1837) at his death in 1883 left a bequest to the college of $83,000 plus a library of over 4000 volumes. There being no proper place in the college to house the books, they were initially kept in rooms rented from the Historical and Scientific Society of Manitoba. From 1890 to 1898 they were kept at the McIntyre Block and were destroyed by fire in 1898. A major collection of rare early Bibles and Anglican religious books was contributed in 1897 by the Vicar of St. Paul's, Whitechapel, the Reverend Daniel Greatorex. The library also received copies of most of the many books being translated into First Nations languages by Anglican missionaries. But there was no collection policy and little money for the purchase of new books. Regrettably, many of these early donations have been destroyed or dispersed, although the Greatorex Collection was deposited by St. John's College in the Rare Book Room of Dafoe Library in February 1979.

If students were not to be found in the library, however, they were to be found in student organizations and especially on the playing fields. The participation rate in sports and other student activities was remarkably high, although of course this was an era in which people were accustomed to making their own amusements and entertainment. Rugby football was the leading college sport, with a five-team league organized in 1888 consisting of Manitoba College, St. John's College, the medical college, the normal school, and the graduates. St. John's College won the first cup. Track and field went intercollegiate about the same time, and was followed in the early 1890s by hockey, curling, and basketball. Non-competitive (i.e., not part of intercollegiate) sports included cricket, tennis, and snowshoeing. All the sports contests were well attended by students, who cheered their teams and athletes on to victory. A college "athletic sports" day was held every year in late May for both the school and the college. The events consisted mainly of track and field competitions, although such unorthodox tests of strength as "throwing cricket ball" were also on the program.

Two St. John's College rugby cheers of the 1890s, as reported in the college literary magazine, were:

Che-He, Che-Ha, Che-Ha-Ha-Ha,
St. John's, St. John's,—Rah! Rah! Rah!

Rickedydick, Rickedydick, Rickedydick Rue
We are St. John's College—Who are You?

Athletic championships were routinely factored together with student academic medals as ways of measuring the comparative achievements of the colleges. Manitoba College and St. John's College were the most frequent winners and were bitter rivals. A return rugby match between St. John's College and Manitoba College in 1889 had turned particularly nasty. Sometime before the turn of the century, reported one observer, the popular conception of a "college man" shifted from one of a near-sighted individual carrying a load of books to "a husky fellow in a padded suit with a rugby ball under his arm." The shift was part of the emergence of the ideal of "muscular Christianity," with its emphasis on the cultivation of character, fair play, and "honest, manly sport." No Canadian was more responsible for this image than Winnipeg's Rev. C.W. Gordon, who as "Ralph Connor" wrote a series of best-selling novels in the early years of the century that fully illustrated it. Gordon was a Presbyterian rather than an Anglican, a Manitoba College rather than a St. John's College man, but the pre-war world he documented encompassed both institutions.

In 1893 Bishop Machray was honoured by his church by becoming elevated as primate of all Canada and archbishop of Rupert's Land. The increased responsibilities contributed to health problems beginning in 1894, which led him to withdraw somewhat from the daily hands-on administration of St. John's College he had carried on since 1866. In early May 1898 a special meeting of St. John's College council was held to "consider the attitude of the College in regards to the establishment of a University Faculty of Science & questions related thereto." Archbishop Machray was not present. Dean O'Meara explained that the Dominion had offered a site at the driving park, a prominent open space on Broadway in downtown Winnipeg, for a university building. After much discussion the council agreed that the location of such a building would lead to material suffering on the part of the college, but it could not bring itself to oppose directly such a gift. A few weeks later a much better attended meeting, with the chancellor in the chair, agreed to address a protest to the chancellor and council of the university, which complained that the proposed site was five kilometres distant from St. John's College. The acceptance of this free gift would "disturb the harmony & break up the unity of the University." The college council added that it had supported the establishment of a professoriate in the university, both for its general advantages and for its special advantages to St. John's College "in being set free from an effort for a full staff in Arts, which has weighed heavily on other Church of England Colleges in Canada having University powers." But to locate the campus downtown would negate these advantages by forcing St. John's to duplicate the university lectures.

Despite the objections by St. John's College (and St. Boniface College), construction was begun on the science building in 1899, and it was completed in 1901. Located near the York Avenue end of the site, the building was made of brick and four storeys high. The ground floor contained two lecture theatres capable of holding 150 students each, plus laboratories. The second floor had more classrooms, a conservatory, a library, and a council chamber seating 100. The basement had six more rooms, and a room for bicycles. The top floor was not initially utilized. During construction, the big question revolved around when the province would allow the university to take over teaching from the colleges. A collateral question was whether all the colleges would actually stop teaching in arts and sciences when the university had its own faculty and curriculum. The ultimate fading away of the colleges, at least the Protestant ones, had been implicit in the early years. But more than a generation of being expected, virtually required, to mount a university-level program, gave the colleges a vested interest in higher education that some would find difficult to surrender totally.

The complaints from St. John's College about the science building's location were met by allowing St. John's students tram fare from Main Street to downtown, a practice that would continue for over twenty years. Why this building was more difficult for Johnians to reach than the earlier rental rooms is not clear. Almost everybody (except St. Boniface College) agreed that a single university on a single site was the eventual goal, but by the turn of the century that goal was becoming increasingly abstract and difficult to achieve. In practical terms, within the colleges there was considerable disagreement over the question of location, over the method of administration, and over the division of teaching faculties, all of which would hold matters up for years. During the protracted period of uncertainty, it was difficult for the colleges to raise money or to plan for the future. A major fundraising campaign was mounted by Manitoba College in 1900, on the grounds that all arts teaching fell to the colleges and would continue to do so for the foreseeable future.

The years between 1901 and 1910 represent a period in which great change might have come to St. John's College—but did not. At the turn of the century, the opportunity for the province to take over control of higher education at the University of Manitoba from the denominational colleges was clearly present. A number of new constituencies had emerged with new demands and fresh needs. Some of those interests were occupational; some were geographical. In the best interests of everybody, the provincial assumption of the control of higher education should have been swift and complete. The introduction of a full secular university based in Winnipeg would have enabled all of the component parts of the system—actual and potential, throughout the province—to adjust simultaneously to the new arrangements. Instead, the province moved in incremental steps toward a provincial university, spending much of the first decade of the twentieth century sidetracked by such matters as the establishment of an agricultural college and by the question of the location of both agricultural college and university, rather than turning its money—and its energies—to the creation of a full-fledged university teaching institution. The failure of the province to act decisively to create a full-fledged provincial university was a many-headed disaster, its consequences spreading in all directions for many years.

The reasons for the failure of foresight and decisiveness in higher education, particularly around the turn of the twentieth century, remain one the great mysteries of the history of Manitoba. No single factor stands out. Instead, a variety of countervailing considerations appear to have paralyzed a succession of governments. The rural districts tended to be both anti-intellectual and hostile to Winnipeg. They could be served by the creation of an agricultural college. Moreover, catering to Winnipeg might lead other aspiring cities to demand their own facilities, once the province took over responsibility for higher education. The experiences of the Manitoba Schools Question made some politicians reluctant to offend the francophone (and Catholic) minority by introducing secular higher education. Gradually, competition among rival groups of land speculators to locate educational facilities on their sites within Winnipeg became added into the equation. Most of all, however, the province was stingy. It did not want to become involved in any unnecessary expenses, and the establishment of a provincially funded public university would obviously be a major financial commitment.

In retrospect, it is easy to see that the denominational colleges that in 1900 still constituted the University of Manitoba needed to be more proactive, deciding on what they wanted to become when a secular state-supported university finally came into full existence rather than responding with half-measures of support or hostility to each hesitant new step on the part of the provincial government. Had the colleges been able to agree on what their ultimate role or roles within the full university would be, they could have worked toward those goals and left the province to work out its own university destiny. Even if the colleges could not agree, they could individually have decided where they wanted to end up and worked toward that target, whatever that was. In the event, only the Catholic francophone community had any clear sense of direction, and it was distinctly negative. It did not want to become subsumed into a secular English-speaking university, which meant that St. Boniface College would fight to retain its own existence, regardless of what the other colleges decided.

For St. John's College, the first half-dozen years of the twentieth century ought to have been ones of enormous uncertainty as regards the college's future direction. But one searches the council minutes in vain before 1907 for much sign of discussion of the great issues facing the college. In 1901, for example, the council recorded more than ten pages worth of discussion revising the theological curriculum, and one sentence approving a committee to cooperate with the synod on "gaining information as to available sites for the College in the City." The question of a new college site from time to time appeared on the agenda of council for the next few years, but the minutes offered few details. Part of the problem of lack of vision may have been that the college council during these years was composed almost exclusively of clergymen, who were neither familiar with the secular issues of the day nor connected with the inner circles of the governments of Manitoba. Before late October 1905, virtually the only laymen from the outside community attending council meetings were Sheriff Inkster, who by this time was out of touch with current politics, and Mr. Heber Archibald, a prominent local attorney. At that time, T. Mayne Daly from Portage, a principal bagman of the Conservative Party, was added to the council, but he did not attend meetings on a regular basis. Part of the problem may also have been an absence of direction from the top, as Warden Machray was ill in the years before his death and Archbishop Matheson could hardly give full attention to the college in the midst of all his other duties and responsibilities. In any case, the college drifted during a period fraught with change.

As a result, moving the college from its Main Street location to a site with more accommodation closer to the university buildings and some of the other colleges appears to have been the principal response of St. John's College to all the changes of the early years of the century. Archbishop Matheson told the 1906 diocesan synod: "We are painfully handicapped for room in our present college, and the growth of both college and school is being hindered by our present circumstances." Lack of accommodation was the college cry of the time. This was hardly out of keeping with the boom mentality of Winnipeg in the early years of the twentieth century, but it did not take into account the possibility that the university, when properly established, would or should take students away from the colleges. The earlier hope of Archbishop Machray that St. John's College would be allowed to concentrate on theological education when the university came into full existence was no longer heard in college discussions. But at the same time, how the college would actually fit into the new scheme of things was hardly very clear, either.

In 1901 Premier Rodmond Roblin appointed a Royal Commission to investigate the establishment of an agricultural college. A year later this Royal Commission reported that farmers needed professional instruction. It argued: "Your Commissioners think that education in agriculture for young men from the rural districts, should be so given by a separate college, that they may not be side-tracked or alienated from the farm." This concept of a physically separate agricultural college would become a powerful—and usually negative—force in the history of the development of the university, considerably more influential than that of the denominational colleges. The commission allowed that the agricultural college could be affiliated with the University of Manitoba, but did not feel any responsibility for the fact that the University of Manitoba still did not have much existence apart from the denominational colleges. The new college would have two departments, agriculture for men and domestic science for women, and operate from November to March. A site of 100 to 200 acres would be required, apart from an experimental farm. As a result the government purchased a site of 117 acres on the south bank of Assiniboine River in what was to become Tuxedo. For its part, the college council early in 1902 debated the asphalting of Main Street North and appointed a committee to object to the improvements. One reason for the objections was the cost resulting from a substantial frontage tax on the college property, which abutted Main Street for some distance.

The gradual process by which the University of Manitoba emerged from the "republic of colleges" produced all manner of problems and casualties. In 1900, amendments to the University Act had allowed the university for the first time the power to appoint and dismiss professors. In 1902, the death of Dean O'Meara forced a general revision of the St. John's College faculty of theology. A motion appended to this reorganization called for a resident master to teach "French & German, & perhaps Elementary Science," at a salary of about $800. The individual eventually appointed (at $700 per annum) did not have any science credentials. This hiring was followed later in 1902 by the formal appointment of the three science instructors of the colleges as half-time university lecturers in natural science, each receiving $1000 a year for their services. The action apparently came under the earlier amendments to the University Act, and it was not even rubber-stamped by the college council. Although the move was clearly only a stop-gap measure, which was not to continue when permanent appointments were made, it led to expectations for the future on the part of at least some of the three men appointed, which would not be fulfilled. That same year the city of Brandon complained about the failure of the university to hold examinations beyond the matriculation level in centres outside Winnipeg. Brandon had a denominational college run by the Baptists, but the denomination would not permit it to affiliate with a provincial institution receiving state support. The petition complained that every member of the university council resided in Winnipeg and that the council was run by the four denominational colleges of Winnipeg. This was true, although it suggested some of the existing hostility to the present university arrangement.

The simple solutions to Brandon's problem were affiliation and a general policy of allowing examinations outside Winnipeg; these were adopted in 1903. Not all university problems were so easily resolved, however. When the Manitoba Medical College in 1903 petitioned for a site on the university grounds, this request could not easily be granted without defining the relationship between the affiliated colleges and the university, but to do this before having figured out what the university was going to look like was extremely difficult. St. John's College by 1903 was again in financial difficulty, and the council passed an increase in tuition fees and in boarding charges. It also passed a motion "that the College Board be authorised to procure assistance if necessary to carry on the College Work," although it is not clear from the minutes exactly what this meant. One of the fundraising schemes involved the subdivision into building lots of the old college playground. The college also sold cemetery lots in a "new St. John's Cemetery." It would raise the price of lots in 1905 to $7.50 per foot and also restrict their purchase to members of the Church of England. In the college, the year 1903 also saw the election of the Reverend Walter Burman as bursar and steward of St. John's College and the college school. In addition, Burman would lecture in botany and on the English Bible. His salary for this assortment of duties would be $700 per annum.

The year 1904 saw a number of moves with regard to higher education in Manitoba. The university organized a faculty of science with six professorships funded mainly by Lord Strathcona, who gave $20,000, payable over four years. Five scientists were imported from outside the province (A.H. Buller in botany and geology, Frank Allen in physics and minerology, M.A. Parker in chemistry, R.R. Cochrane in mathematics, Swale Vincent in physiology and biology) and the sixth appointment was made to Gordon Bell, the provincial bacteriologist, whose salary continued to be paid by the province. The scientists based in the colleges who had been given half-time appointments in 1902 were overlooked and bypassed in this expansion, which involved the appointment of individuals parachuted into Manitoba with impressive credentials at internationally competitive salaries. St. John's College's Edgar Kenrick was particularly unhappy with his treatment.

As a result of the new appointments, the University of Manitoba now consisted of a number of denominational arts colleges, a college of medicine, and a relatively high-powered faculty of science. The new scientists brought with them a quite different set of academic values, nurtured not at all in the commons rooms of Oxbridge colleges but in the seminar rooms of German and English red-brick universities. Specialized post-graduate training was the new norm, and the scientists were committed to research, scholarship, and publication on the international stage. As well as the college image of the young man with the rugby ball, there was now also a university image of a young man with a laboratory coat and a test tube in his hand.

The newcomers also brought with them a considerable hostility to religious influence in higher education. A.H. Buller, for example, would later describe the university council as an institution "controlled by a small number whose chief interest does not lie in its true progress, but to that of the affiliated denominational colleges." Given their commitment to publication, the newly appointed scientists represented a quite different conception of higher education for the province, one with which the university council was not in much sympathy. The science appointments helped create a gulf between the university and the colleges based on the familiar "research versus teaching" dichotomy that would become an important component of academic culture of the University of Manitoba for many years and would eventually contribute to the takeover of the colleges by the university in 1970.

Also in 1904, the Manitoba legislature voted $100,000 for an agricultural college, the Manitoba Agricultural College was created by statute, and building began on a site in Tuxedo. The agricultural college's new buildings were completed in 1906 at a cost of $250,000. No difficulties about funding existed when it came to the province's farmers. They were an identifiable political constituency that needed to be wooed. But then, the denominational colleges had absolutely no stake in agricultural and home economics courses. At the same time that Lord Strathcona had endowed the faculty of science at the university, he also provided $15,000 for St. John's College, two-thirds to be added to the endowment fund and $5000 for the purchase of a new site. In its acknowledgement of this gift, the college council noted that some of the money had been used "to purchase from the H.B.Co. of a most desirable site for the contemplated new College Building near the university." The college decided to mount a public campaign for the "new College." It appointed a canvasser (Rev. W.J. Garton, rector of Morden) at a salary of $1500 per year, as well as necessary travelling and office expenses. Late in 1905 the college was offered the balance of the block between Osborne and Colony streets as an addition to the new college site, but council decided the money involved was "excessive."

In April 1904, Archbishop Machray had died. Until two years before his death, he had taught higher mathematics at the college, and served both as chancellor and warden for many years until his demise. While in earlier years Machray had been a positive force in the college, in his last years he had by his very presence stood in the way of major reform. The speed with which, after his death, the council moved to instal electric light in the college building suggests that Machray had been opposed to such innovation. Machray was succeeded as archbishop and chancellor by Samuel Matheson and as warden by Dean Coombes. His generosity to the college continued beyond his death, with a bequest of $12,500 to the endowment fund.

In late 1905 and early 1906, the recently arrived Dr. Buller (of the new faculty of science) wrote a series of articles for the *Manitoba Free Press* advocating that the university expand and move from its Broadway location to a site in Tuxedo near the agricultural college. These articles were the opening salvo in a reinvigorated debate over the future of the university. St. John's College council participated in this debate; the council minutes for 9 November 1906 recorded "some discussion took place on the question of the policy of the University as it affects the college," but there is no further elaboration of what was said. At the same meeting it was recorded that the college building fund had collected to date $20,470 and expended $5082 (some for taxes). A meeting in May 1907 disclosed additional collections of twenty-two dollars, suggesting that the building fund had stalled badly. But it had recovered late in the year, so that the fundraiser in the November 1907 *St. John's College Magazine* reported subscriptions of $66,550, with $29,573 already paid. That same issue of the college magazine contained an article observing that female students had virtually disappeared from the "ladies parlour" of the college. This observation might well have led the authorities to question their assumption of the unlimited potential for growth, but apparently it did not. Fortunately, the shortage of female students corrected itself over the next few years.

The college council meeting of May 1907 passed a motion to appoint a committee to meet with representatives of the other colleges to discuss an agreement among them about the university site. Also in 1907, a committee of the university council reported university expansion, recommending the establishment of departments of engineering with three chairs, plus the introduction of departments of history, political economy, law, and modern languages. These recommendations challenged the colleges by entering into liberal arts teaching for the first time. Not all the colleges were hostile. St. Boniface and Wesley wanted to retain the traditional structure of the "republic of colleges." For its part, St. John's College favoured that the university take up teaching in every department as soon as funds should allow. The college also insisted that the university needed a mixture of colleges, denominational and secular, on a common site. Canon J.O. Murray of St. John's argued at a public banquet that "the right solution of the question was that the University should undertake a higher form of University work, and that the colleges should do tutorial and individual work." One Manitoba College alumnus responded to the proposals for a university by observing, "when the university is prepared to take up teaching in all the Arts branches, then the colleges will gladly acquiesce, and confine their attention solely to teaching theology. But until that time the colleges will be inclined to remain where they are and continue the splendid work which they are doing."

In the summer of 1907 a great step forward was taken in the college library, when, for the first time, the books in it were properly classified and catalogued, using the "latest Dewey & Cutter system." Circulars were sent to former students requesting the return of any college books they still had in their possession; the success of this program of recovery is not known.

The *St. John's College Magazine,* which resumed publication after a four-year hiatus in the autumn of 1907, not only proudly reported on the library, but also on the three Johnians—Stewart Beech, C.A. Adamson, and A.H. Miller—who were studying at Oxford as Rhodes Scholars.

As a result of the disagreements over all aspects of the future of higher education, another committee of the university council reported that the government should appoint a commission of inquiry to examine the constitution and management of the university, its assets and finances, the connection between the university and its colleges, the scope of teaching at the university, and its site and buildings. This commission was chaired by J.A.M. (always known to his friends as "Jam") Aikins, a prominent Winnipeg businessman and later lieutenant-governor of the province. It heard fourteen deputations and individual members visited the University of Toronto, McGill, Laval, Minnesota, Northwestern, Michigan, and Illinois. While the commission was deliberating, the Tuxedo Park Company, through an open letter to the press, offered to donate 150 acres for the university on the southern boundary of Assiniboine Park, opposite the south entrance. Arthur Buller later boasted that he had personally chosen the site and pushed the scheme "to the utmost of my ability." He was probably at least partly motivated by real estate speculation; everyone was in those days. The council liked the site, but held off a decision until the commission had finally reported.

A subsequent St. John's College council meeting in June 1907 discussed a letter from Mr. Heubach, the promoter who had offered the site in Tuxedo for the university, enquiring whether St. John's College would move to such a site were the university to build on it. The college decided to write to the university council that while it already had a new site next to the existing university structure on Broadway, it had not yet commenced building upon it. The college was still "free to make a change," but it urged a speedy decision on the matter so that college construction could commence. At a meeting in September 1907, the college council expressed the view that the university needed a larger site near the centre of the city, but failing such a site, the one in Tuxedo should be accepted. Late in 1907 an order-in-council affiliated the Manitoba Agricultural College with the university, but the agricultural college would soon be on the move from its Tuxedo location.

St. John's College council responded on 19 December 1907 to a draft report from the commission on higher education with a lengthy position paper, which it would subsequently amend and submit to the commission. This paper appeared as if from nowhere on the council minutes, although obviously its preparation had involved considerable prior discussion. Most of the paper was typed and there were a number of crossing-outs and interlineations, probably reflecting changes made when the document was discussed. The contents of the document as well as its appearance deserve a careful scrutiny, since it reflects the college's considered responses to most of the contentious issues of the new century. It started with the site question, insisting that a larger site than the present one on Broadway was required. Additional buildings would be necessary for engineering, the physical sciences, a new museum, and library, as well as an examination hall suitable for the conferring of degrees. The council insisted that space between the buildings was required to "enhance their architectural beauty" and that the design of the buildings should be a point of pride for the province. A site of at least 150 acres would be required, and the Tuxedo site was acceptable if no other nearer the city was to be found. As for funding, the council wanted the province to provide all the money required for carrying on the work of the university, adopting the methods of financing used in the United States or at the University of Toronto. The council was certain that the taxpayers could be "educated to appreciate the advantage to the Province as a whole of a properly equipped University." The new institution should have a proper full-time president and a board of governors as at the University of Toronto, and a more representative senate. The college council could even conceive of the representation of the affiliated colleges being reduced, particularly if the university took over the teaching in arts.

The council took the view that the university should offer instruction in all branches of higher education, leaving the colleges "free to supplement such teaching in whatever way they desire." The St. John's College position was that the present system in which each college offered instruction in arts multiplied staffs and was unsatisfactory. The council rejected a system of intercollegiate cooperation for arts teaching, observing that it would be unstable and would not resolve the "fundamental requirement of all successful university work," which was "that the Professors should be men whose main interest and sole professional duty are the study and teaching of the subjects which they profess, and who have time and opportunity for research." The council argued that students who belonged to denominations not maintaining colleges or to no denomination should not have to enrol in denominational colleges. Moreover, an invidious distinction would be introduced between science and arts subjects if science were provided by the university and arts by the colleges. But the council really stressed the inequity to the colleges of saddling them with the burden of "giving the only teaching provided for in Arts Courses of the Provincial University." Special provision could be made for French-speaking students, and mental and moral science should remain with the colleges. The council concluded its answer by emphasizing the need for "one University for the Province."

In an appendix approved in early January 1908, the college council observed that it had consistently opposed the downtown site, but had finally decided to procure an adjacent lot of land in order to be able to afford the university's advantages to its students. But it became increasingly doubtful that the Broadway site was adequate for expansion, leading the college to postpone building. The result was that the college was being "prevented from developing its prestige in the estimation of many of its ardent supporters" who did not understand the site situation. Council added that the connection between affiliated colleges and university should be maintained; coordination would work best, it wrote, if each college had its own special place in the university system. The affiliated colleges should be represented on the senate of the university. Moreover, if arts colleges, they should have the right "to send up students without their being required to pass the matriculation Examinations," and the students of such affiliated colleges should be allowed to substitute college courses for university ones under proper regulations.

At first glance, the college's position at the beginning of 1908 on the various aspects of the university question seemed clear enough. It wanted a larger site as well as full public funding in arts, science, and any other branches of higher education. It not only favoured university instruction in arts, but suggested at this point that it did not wish to involve itself in arts teaching in any subject in which it did not have appropriate full-time professional faculty. Some of the items on this shopping list were contradictory, and, unfortunately, what the college actually wanted was not all that transparent. It would be possible to understand that what the St. John's College council intended by the comment about professional faculty was that it was satisfied with the prevailing distinction between senior-level and junior-level work, with the colleges continuing introductory teaching but deferring specialized teaching to the university. Unfortunately, the appendix of early 1908 considerably muddied the waters even on this point. In 1908 the college said it wanted to "send up students"—presumably to the university—without matriculation examinations, but in the Manitoba system matriculation occurred before university work began. This statement obviously dealt with St. John's College School students, rather than with college students proper. The next statement about students being allowed to substitute college courses for university ones, however, indicated that the college might not be thinking only about first- and second-year courses for itself, but about upper-level work in some disciplines. In fairness to the college council, the final resolution of many of these issues could only be made after the province had determined its course of action. But St. John's position at this time seemed to point the future post-university curriculum either in the direction of continuation of the first two years of the arts component of the college as a sort of junior college or of the continuation of a four-year program in certain disciplines, or both.

By the time of the comprehensive college report in 1907–08, the number of organizations and activities at the college was much expanded over the situation in the 1890s. The vibrancy of the extramural life undoubtedly made increasingly difficult the proposition of reduction of the student body solely to theologues. The annual Commemoration Day now included a football (rugby) game between the alumni and the "Present," as well as a musical concert. The rugby club celebrated its twenty-first anniversary with a banquet at the Royal Alexandra Café. A chess club, a full-fledged intercollegiate debating program (the title was won by St. John's College every year from 1903 to 1907), the St. John's College Dramatic Society, as well as a church society and the Brotherhood of St. Andrew's (a missionary group that met alternate Fridays in the college library), had been added to the older events and clubs, such as the literary society. Women became actively involved in many of these clubs and activities, although not the theological ones. There was even a women's hockey team organized in 1908, which played the senior school team on 16 March. The college magazine confessed that "most of the girls had never played before," but had gotten better with practice; the women's hockey team would defeat a team from the boys' school in 1909 by a score of seven to four, and follow up that victory with one over a team from Wesley College. The college magazine not only published a photograph, but a poem:

> Some one once had pretty feet
>   All clad in silken hose,
> And shod in dainty glace kid
>   With patent leather toes.
> But now a change has taken place,
>   Most painful to repeat;
> Shin-guards encase her ankles slim,
>   And square-toed boots her feet.
> Some one used to dress her hair
>   The most artistic way
> In little curls and rippling waves,
>   Tied up with ribbons gay.
> But now she draws it tightly back,
>   And puts it in a net,
> And looks to me absurdly like
>   A third-rate suffragette.

> Now if these dire calamities
>   Are all to hockey due,
> This forfeiting of charm and grace,
>   And of complexion too;
> The inartistic mode of dress
>   And hair devoid of curl,
> Then may the fates preserve me from
>   The hockey-playing girl.

In 1908, a women's basketball team made its first appearance. Two years later, hockey enthusiasm among the women was replaced by excitement about curling. Curiously enough, the female students at St. John's College in 1908 also discussed the possibility of imitating Manitoba College in establishing a literary society "for ladies only," thus contemplating segregation rather than integration by gender. The new sport introduced in 1909 was the "paper chase," held over a sixteen-kilometre course along the river. Hazing for freshmen still flourished. An article in the college magazine in November 1909 reported that those who had stigmatized "Initiation" as dangerous and foolish had been routed, and a night of "initiation still holds its own in the college." It added, "a promise to do better in the future, exacted amid the terrors of such a night, has often been the means of turning a 'freshy' from being a nuisance or a drone into a useful member of the college." The first Varsity dance was held at Manitoba Hall late in 1909. Despite the ongoing uncertainty over the future of higher educational policy in the province, these years were the "golden age" of student extracurricular activity, not just for St. John's College but for all the component parts of the University of Manitoba. In general St. John's College more or less held its own in intramural competitions in sports and such other matters as debating, although as the decade wore on, the victories for "Toba" (Manitoba College) became more frequent.

Although there was still no report from the commission of inquiry, the university agreed in 1909 to appoint chairs in political economy, English, and history; teaching in these subjects was to be limited to third- and fourth-year arts students. Students had been active in lobbying for appointments in these disciplines, especially in English and history. When these appointments were actually made later in the year, a faculty of arts and science was in effect created, although the only faculty was called the university faculty. Both because the disciplines involved did not cover all the arts teaching and because teaching was to be limited to upper-level students only, the colleges were not yet supplanted and still maintained a critical role in the process of higher education.

The *St. John's College Magazine* in 1908 complained that "amongst our undergraduates on the one hand, the university spirit is kept too subservient to that of the college, and among the general public on the other, there is a lack of interest in this momentous question sufficient to cause some misgiving." A year later, in June 1909, the student magazine editorialized in defence of the college from complaints in synod that members of the college were not winning their fair share of academic honours. The editorial pointed out the inadequacy of measurement by "pot-hunting," and concluded by observing: "In comparison with other local colleges, St. John's is heavily handicapped and must remain so until the policy of the University becomes settled." Why the magazine thought St. John's peculiarly disadvantaged was not made clear. The reference may have been to uncertainty over where to build. Alternatively, the problem may have been that by the end of 1909, the building fund had collected only $38,343 and had only another $31,000 promised, which meant that the fund had grown very slowly. In any event, the college magazine explained, "it is only the uncertainty regarding the site of the new university that is preventing the foundations of the new college being laid." A committee of the college council met with the premier, Sir Rodmond Roblin, and two of his ministers late in 1909 to discuss the question of the university site, but reported back to council that it had learned nothing; the government "gave them a sympathetic hearing but could hold out as definite no prospect of anything being done in the immediate future."

The St. John's College student magazine was certainly unequivocally clear in its call for the creation of a proper university. A subsequent issue of the magazine early in 1910 insisted that the earlier view of the synod meeting was "strange," and denied that the performance of its students had been discussed, claiming that what was under discussion was the attitude of people in the diocese. The editor then proceeded to print a separate article detailing "the relation of St. John's College to the Synod of the Diocese." This piece insisted, "whatever reason may be assigned by Churchmen of the Diocese for their lack of interest in their College, the statement should never be made, or if made should be promptly corrected, that the College is not under the control of the Diocese." Everyone was waiting for the royal commission to report. The *St. John's College Magazine* insisted that there was demand for a state-controlled university, and added that public opinion had shown the commission what it wanted. The magazine even offered an opinion in verse in its November 1909 issue:

> To the University Commission
> [italics in the original]
> *Oh! when the craze for commissions came West;*
> *And Manitoba decided that it was for the best;*
> *When men were appointed and articles written,*
> *When lecturers spoke and students were smitten,*
> *When Westbrook compiled the facts and the figures,*
> *When Drummond dismissed them with eloquent gestures,*
> *When the "Meds" they decided that willing they'd be*
> *To move from their site—yea, e'en to the sea;*
> *When "Toba" they wavered, and Wesley said "No,"*
> *When the hearts of St. John's were all in a glow—*
> *A commission was founded by royal command,*
> *And the sound triumphed forth like Flaherty's band.*
> *Since then we have missed it, and gaze still in vain,*
> *O'er turret and tower, o'er prairie and plain.*
> *Oh, give us news, and our longings appease,*
> *And let us decide what we dare not conceive;*
> *That it died—what! felo-de-se!*
> *Or drowned in the depths of political sea.*

The report of the commission of enquiry was finally tabled in the legislature early in 1910. The *St. John's College Magazine* had insisted late in 1909, "The commision can not, if it would, submit a narrow weak report." But the seven commissioners could not agree, and as a result there were three reports that collectively added up to a weak one. A minority report signed by Aikins and Rev. A.A. Cherrier of St. Boniface wanted a traditional university dominated by the denominational colleges, with little government control. The other two reports wanted a full state-supported university managed by a board of governors on a large site, with a president, expanded teaching departments, and room for the colleges to teach what they wanted. The vital difference of opinion, said the report, "was as to whether the denominational colleges should have representation upon any of the governing bodies of the University and the extent and character of that representation." This assertion was not quite accurate, for there was also disagreement over the site, with the majority wanting a larger site and the minority more land near Broadway, as well as over the extent of subsidization of arts teaching in the colleges.

While none of the reports were informed by any consistent philosophy of higher education beyond utilitarianism, all three reports wanted the financial and business administration of the university separated from the academic and administered by "men of affairs" rather than by academics, as the St. John's College council had recommended in 1907. Significantly, none of the reports had any vision of the colleges as integral parts of the university or any notion of colleges as liberal arts institutions. At best the colleges were seen as interim institutions until the province could decide on its priorities. The report itself argued, "the greater body of education lies and must ever lie outside of higher Arts courses. It is connected with the utilities and vocations. . . . Without such higher and special instruction Canada will never take its place among the nations of the world as an industrial and commercial leader." This echo of the sort of talk circulating around the British Association of the Advancement of Science meetings in Winnipeg in 1909 was symptomatic of the times. The association's meetings in Winnipeg were themselves an illustration of Winnipeg boosterism, and they offered weeks of papers and lectures on the great gains and advantages being made on all fronts by science of all kinds.

All the parties to the report favoured an American-style, provincial, full-service university as the ultimate choice for Manitoba, but nobody offered either timetable or sequence of events for getting to the goal. Equally importantly, the report was not very clear about the nature of provincial financial support. The commission report obviously resolved very little. The Wesley College board of governors found it so equivocal that they decided to press ahead with a new downtown building. The university council rejected a draft university bill that did not call for a full state-controlled university and voted in favour of the earlier preferred Tuxedo site at about the same time that the provincial government decided to purchase a new site for the agricultural college. The inside story of this decision to move the agricultural school to a new location has never been told, and probably cannot ever be reconstructed out of the subterranean internal manoeuvring. Possibly the government wanted the agricultural school to be physically separate from the university; probably it was reacting negatively to the pressure of the Tuxedo developers. The official reason was that there was not enough room for animals and an experimental farm at Tuxedo. The province would eventually choose a site of 570 acres on an oxbow of the Red River in the outer reaches of St. Vital, beginning the construction of new buildings there in 1911. Whether it intended to allow the university to take over the abandoned buildings in Tuxedo is not clear.

The complications and confusions of the site issue loom like a grey cloud over higher education in these years. No one understood the question fully at the time, and it has been almost impossible to unravel it since. Basically, there would eventually emerge three possible sites for the university: Broadway, Tuxedo, and Fort Garry, and the colleges found themselves for some years required to locate their own buildings in ignorance of which university site would eventually be chosen. Some colleges wanted to remain physically clear of the university; others wanted to be as close to it as possible. In the wake of the university council decision for the Tuxedo site, the St. John's College Magazine insisted that the acceptance of the Heubach site had a number of drawbacks: first, it "throws the University into the arms of the real estate dealers"; secondly, it was not big enough, particularly since its 117 acres could not be compared with Saskatchewan's 1172 acres;

third, it was not river frontage; and finally, the decision did not guarantee proper planning. The magazine advocated holding "what we have," i.e., the site on Osborne. At the same time it also editorialized in favour of a single university. This goal was partly motivated by such considerations as the examination problems of the federated system, in which students wrote on papers set by professors who had not taught them and whom they had never seen nor heard. But there was also a larger vision: "there must come a broader social feeling, a feeling that while each man may belong to a certain College, all are members of one University, for the interests of which all personal emotions must be sunk or set aside."

In the summer 1910 issue of the *St. John's College Magazine,* associate editor A.D. Baker (who lectured in "moderns" at the college) offered an editorial entitled "Our Position." The writer recognized the right questions: "where do we stand as a college?" and "what are we doing to take our true place in the new and larger university that is to be?" Unfortunately he waffled on the answers. If one had faith in the college, Baker wrote, one had to believe that "its place in the new and larger university will be even more important than its present position in the body corporate." This new importance was reflected in part in the building fund campaign for the new college building. Internally, each part of the college must be "strengthened, vitalized." This meant that each overburdened member of faculty needed to work harder, to teach better, and to attend all meetings. There should be a new administrator, a resident warden, who gave his whole time to the institution, while the college council should recognize "the crisis now upon us." While the college had rich spiritual equipment to contribute to a university, its material appointments lagged behind those of other institutions and needed to be enhanced. Among the material needs, the college council was told early in 1910, were an ice rink and a gymnasium that could serve as a drill hall. The college at this time was contemplating disciplined exercise and drilling of students rather than full-scale military drilling. The sentiments of the author were all useful ones, but did not address in detail the question of precisely what kind of educational institution

St. John's College should become in a new university with its own full-time staff recruited in accordance with modern academic principles.

On 4 November 1910, at a well-attended meeting of the university council, a motion was adopted affirming the principle that the university should be empowered to teach in all subjects and supporting the recommendations on teaching in the two reports of the university commission, which called for the introduction of full teaching by the university. Six votes were cast against the resolutions for full teaching. They came from St. Boniface College and Wesley College, who threatened to withdraw from the university if the proposal were carried. An editorial in the *St. John's College Magazine* in December 1910 pointed out that the objections of St. Boniface and Wesley were based on the assertion that the colleges would be reduced to a secondary role, and insisted that such objections were not warranted by the proposed change. There was no prospect that first- and second-year teaching by the colleges was being jeopardized, and even if it were, said this editorial, it would "be a relief." Even if students were sent by a college to university lectures, the colleges still retained the right to teach their own courses. The real issue, announced this writer, was "the fear that students who under existing circumstances would enrol themselves as members of the affiliated colleges would join only the University classes, if provision were made for their instruction by the University." Such a position was neither "dignified" nor "self-respecting." St. John's College did not fear competition, but rather welcomed it. These were admirable sentiments, so long as they did not involve hitching the college's wagon to an increasingly out-of-date Anglican Church and clergy.

At the end of 1910, Prof. Daniel Wilson published a little pamphlet entitled *The Case for Wesley College* in support of a petition for separate degree-granting powers for Wesley if such became necessary to guarantee the autonomy of the college. In his pamphlet Wilson tried to develop a case for the liberal arts college, emphasizing small-group instruction, personal attention, and the development of social attitudes such as "a common bond of fellowship." The public articulation of such a case was confined to Wesley, however, and was not part of the stated thinking of the other colleges, which apparently appeared smugly to believe that their teaching staffs, composed chiefly of clergymen lacking in specialized knowledge, advanced training, and a commitment to scholarship through publication, could at least in the first two years be competitive with a university staff recruited under the new assumptions of higher education. Wesley was the only English-speaking college that gave any sign of seeking to remain autonomous, however. The public response to Wesley's initiative was one of hostility, chiefly on the grounds that separate degree-granting denominational colleges would undermine a strong provincial university by spreading the finances too thin. Where such an attitude left the provincial agricultural college was one matter. Where this attitude left St. John's College is yet another one.

The St. John's College building on the Main Street site of the Cathedral, erected in 1866 and used until 1890. The original building did not include the porches, which were later embellishments.

The young Robert Machray, about the time of his arrival in Red River.

These architect's drawings for the college's proposed new buildings in north Winnipeg (top) clearly show the influence of English models. The building actually completed in 1886 (below) was considerably more modest.

St. John's College staff and some students, 1885. In the top row, far left, is Samuel Matheson, later archbishop and chancellor of the University of Manitoba. Among the students, second from the right (middle row) is the young John Machray, nephew of Archbishop Machray.

Robert Machray, archbishop of Rupert's Land (1895).

The graduating class of 1907, among the first coeducational graduating classes at the college.

The St. John's College Canadian Officers' Training Corps unit (c. 1920). COTC units such as these were a reminder of the influence of WWI on many Canadian campuses.

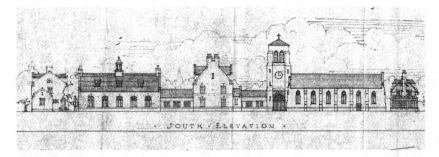

· SOUTH · ELEVATION ·

Architect's drawings for proposed new college buildings at the Fort Garry campus (1932). These buildings were never begun, one of the many victims of the impact of the defalcation.

Rev. Canon George A. Wells, warden from 1921 to 1934.

John Machray (c.1912). What became known as the Machray Defalcation would affect the finances of both the college and the university for decades.

The college's football (rugby) team 1932-33. Future historian W.L. Morton is in the back row, second from the left.

Most Rev. Walter J. Barfoot at the time of his appointment as college warden in 1935. He remained as warden until 1941, and would later play an important role in the college's history as archbishop of Rupert's Land.

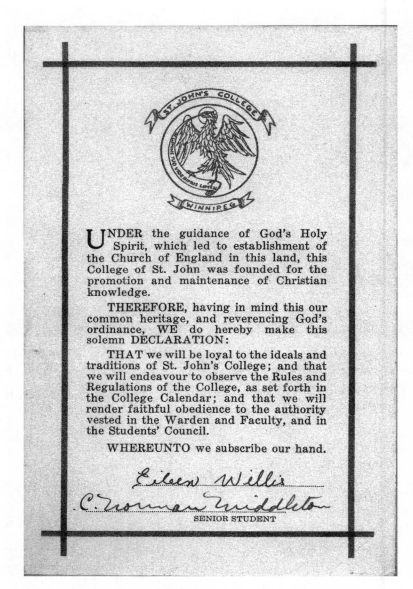

UNDER the guidance of God's Holy Spirit, which led to establishment of the Church of England in this land, this College of St. John was founded for the promotion and maintenance of Christian knowledge.

THEREFORE, having in mind this our common heritage, and reverencing God's ordinance, WE do hereby make this solemn DECLARATION:

THAT we will be loyal to the ideals and traditions of St. John's College; and that we will endeavour to observe the Rules and Regulations of the College, as set forth in the College Calendar; and that we will render faithful obedience to the authority vested in the Warden and Faculty, and in the Students' Council.

WHEREUNTO we subscribe our hand.

Eileen Willis

C. Norman Middleton

SENIOR STUDENT

The college oath taken by college freshmen c. 1932. (courtesy Eileen [Willis] Dill)

Chapter Five

Learning to Live with the University, 1910–1922

THE FIRST PART OF THE SECOND DECADE OF THE TWENTIETH CENTURY
was a time of great uncertainty for higher education in the province. Part
of the trouble was the continued indecision about location, but beyond this
question lurked another: the relationship of the colleges (including the agricultural college) to the expanding university. The province and the city both
boomed somewhat artificially until 1913, and then suffered a severe economic and psychological collapse from which they did not entirely recover
for many years. To some considerable extent, Winnipeg's problem was that
it was rapidly losing its place as the undisputed economic and financial
centre of Canada's prairie West, and certainly St. John's College suffered
along with the city from the constriction, which put a serious crimp in its
fundraising for new construction. Then came the Great War, five years that
would inevitably dominate the life of any institution inhabited chiefly by

young men of military age. The effect of the war had been so devastating that any return to pre-war conditions was almost impossible.

In 1910 and the immediate years afterwards, the possible permutations of site and arrangements with the university seemed virtually endless. Basically, three strategies emerged among the colleges as the university moved into full teaching mode. One strategy was to continue as if the university had not come into existence. This was the choice adopted by St. Boniface College and Wesley College. Another was to give up non-theological teaching to the university. This was the strategy of Manitoba College, which then merged what was left of its operation with Wesley as United College. The third strategy was to attempt to fit a curriculum within the university structure. This would be the choice of St. John's College. This strategy did not require any formal changes to the college curriculum or staff, but merely a realignment of teaching activities. No one could possibly know in 1910 how the Great War would affect any shifts in focus.

The board of Wesley College, like that of St. John's, had eventually, in November 1910, accepted the proposal to move to the site in Tuxedo offered by F.W. Heubach. The Wesley board added, "they were prepared to accept heartily the provision by the Province of instruction even in the subjects now taught by the colleges just as soon as there was a demand for it, and just as soon as the finances of the Province were adequate, provided such instruction be given in a college, under its own separate management and sustaining precisely the same relation to the University as that sustained by the Colleges already in existence." What the Methodists apparently wanted was the creation of another college, this time a secular one. When the Wesley board got no response to this suggestion, it voted in January 1911 in favour of a resolution calling for a petition to the legislature asking for university status for Wesley. Much internal opposition to this proposal existed at the Wesley board, however, and the idea also met with considerable resistance outside the Wesley community. St. John's College council appointed a committee to draft a resolution emphatically opposing "granting degree-conferring powers to any educational body in the Province other than the

University of Manitoba." The resolution spoke about the multiplication of facilities and the consequent lowering of educational standards. The St. John's College was presently responsible in most subjects for teaching in the first and second years, a situation that seemed to satisfy it.

Early 1911 brought a suggestion from "certain friends of the College" that the St. John's College School be established as a boarding school outside the city. The college council discussed the matter fully and decided that not enough information was available upon which to make an immediate decision. The "friends" were invited to consult at the next meeting of council, and on 3 February 1911 a delegation consisting of Messrs. Gardner, Hough, Moss, Chaffe, Robinson, and Dr. Harvey Smith met with the council. This meeting resulted in the appointment of a joint committee of council members and friends to draft a report on the matter. The report, when finally tabled in 1912, called for improvements to the college school on its present site, including a gymnasium and an extended school chapel. The college council subsequently turned down a request for the establishment of a branch school in the south part of the city, but agreed again in 1913 to look into the possibility of moving the school out of the city and was still considering suitable sites outside Winnipeg in 1915.

The year 1911 was regarded as a banner year by the college magazine, for St. John's won the senior intercollegiate hockey championship. The team went undefeated, scoring seventy-seven goals and having only eighteen scored against it, "indeed a splendid record." Apart from hockey, curling also flourished, with a bonspiel that "included every available man in the college." The literary society debated the question whether the college gave too much preference to social organization over scholastic duties, with the winning team maintaining "that the best interests of the College and students can be attained only through Social Organizations in conjunction with Scholastic Duties." The year also brought the publication of a novel by Canon Gill, one of its teaching staff, entitled *Love in Manitoba*, a story of farm life in the Swedish settlement north of Minnedosa. Published authors were rare among faculty members, and the college revelled in Father Gill's success.

The first buildings for the agricultural college on the provincial site at St. Vital (not yet known as Fort Garry) opened in 1911. By 1912 it was clear that the university council and the provincial government did not see eye to eye on the site business. The council continued to be keen for the Tuxedo site, while the government allocated seven acres of space on Broadway Avenue for each of the colleges and offered money for a new engineering building at the same location. Alternately, the province later offered to provide 137 acres between the agricultural college and the university site at St. Vital, on which it would erect and equip an engineering building. That year, the first government amended the Law Society Act (in which the word "person" had been held to refer to men only), and the first two women—Melrose Sissons and Winnifred M. Wilton—were admitted to the law school. Wilton won first prize in the final examinations. At St. John's College the alumni association donated $1500 for three years toward the salary of a college head.

The university council in February 1912, while admitting many unresolved questions, also reported that it had agreed on an imaginative way out of the impasse on university organization. The council wanted a university college, to be known as King's College, which was to be a new secular college with its own faculty and building, teaching certain specified subjects, mainly in the arts. According to W.L. Morton, a later college alumnus, in his history of the university, the plan was scuttled when it was prematurely leaked to the press. What this plan would have meant was that a university college would become another college alongside the existing denominational ones, and instead of those colleges seeing themselves as apart from the university, they would have been enabled to see themselves as part of it.

In the midst of the continued uncertainty over the site for the university, several of the colleges finally decided to engage in building programs. Wesley College constructed near the downtown a building known as the Annex, which would accommodate sixty residential students and 200 in classrooms; in 1917 it became known as Sparling Hall, a residence for women. In 1912, Manitoba College and Wesley College agreed to amalgamate as the United Colleges (later United College), a move that followed some years of teaching cooperation. For its part, the St. John's College council opposed any expenditure of the university endowment upon buildings and threatened to reconsider its acceptance of the Tuxedo site were any new buildings financed out of the endowment. The council on 3 May 1912 discussed a new site for a college building on the corner of Church Avenue and Charles Street, which was approved. The downtown location had obviously been scrapped for the moment, but no reason for the change was ever offered in the council minutes.

St. John's College quickly moved to construct a three-storey residence building on the Church Street property in the North End, close to the present college buildings. It too was called the Annex, and had lecture rooms on the first floor and residences on the upper floors. The construction was scheduled to cost just over $40,000, and the last $10,000 would be financed by the endowment fund on security of the building being completed. Completion of construction was delayed, and according to the college magazine it was regarded as only a temporary expedient until the new college was relocated. In late 1912 the council terminated the appointment of Rev. Garton as collector of the college building fund. The college also offered the office of warden to the Very Reverend John Robinson, who accepted the appointment. The new warden was a graduate of Trinity College, Dublin, where in 1872 he had been a gold medallist in history and political science. He had moved from Belfast to Edmonton in 1911. Students had been most active in the campaign for a resident warden. Students were also actively involved in negotiations for the establishment of university-wide organizations, such as the University Debating Club and university sports teams. By 1912 there was a "Varsity Field Day" and by 1913 a dramatic society.

A number of major developments at the university occurred in 1913 in addition to the creation of the United Colleges and the University Dramatic Society. On 1 January 1913, Dr. James Alexander McLean—formerly of the University of Idaho—took office as the University of Manitoba's first president. A few days thereafter, the university council agreed to talk with the government about the tract of land offered at St. Vital (Fort Garry).

Premier Sir Rodmond Roblin replied that while the government still preferred the Broadway site, it would accept the St. Vital one. The province and the university eventually agreed on St. Vital, a decision applauded by the *St. John's College Magazine.* College lecturer A.D. Baker in the magazine later in 1913 reported that once the agricultural farm had been moved, no doubt had existed in the minds "of the friends of a true state university where the University site should be." The new site was really not much further from downtown than the Tuxedo one, he wrote, and he waxed eloquent on a vision of a "quiet university town" on the banks of the Red River. Baker obviously assumed that the decision for St. Vital would quickly settle the entire university question. But such was not to be. The St. John's College council accepted an offer from the university of a site on the new campus in early 1914, at the same time agreeing to consult with the other affiliated colleges over "the definite terms on which sites should be granted to the Colleges." Meanwhile, the provincial legislature had created "the Manitoba Association of Graduate Nurses" and gave the University of Manitoba the power to conduct examinations in nursing. Internal housekeeping within the college in 1913 saw another recataloguing and rearrangement of the college library. The college magazine still complained that many books were hard to find.

About the same time, the agricultural college withdrew from affiliation with the university in preparation for its move to St. Vital. In the period immediately preceding the start of World War I, there were further developments. In February 1914 the university agreed to take over the pharmacy course begun by the Manitoba Pharmaceutical Association, and in May, the Manitoba Law School—organized by joint agreement of the university and the Law Society of Manitoba—affiliated with the university. Also in February 1914 the St. John's College council agreed to examine the bursar's books "at as reasonable a rate [of time] as possible." In the same year, Manitoba College voted to discontinue its teaching in liberal arts, and turned over its entire student body in arts, plus professors and lecturers, to the university. It also turned its cheers—and its colours, Yale blue on white—over to the new arts faculty of the university. St. John's College did not follow suit, not even when, for its part, the university council agreed to begin teaching a number of subjects for arts degrees in the first and second year, and President J.A. MacLean urged the denominational colleges to give up teaching in arts to the university. As a result, in September 1914 the university—with the nation suddenly at war in Europe—for the first time offered a full arts course. The *St. John's College Magazine* reported in its November 1914 issue on these changes, predicting that the takeover of first- and second-year students by the university would soon result within the college in the confinement of teaching solely to theological training. This did not occur, although the university was also rapidly moving toward a full-service role, with the addition of nursing, pharmacy, and law to its existing professional responsibilities. Unfortunately, as the arts question played itself out, the colleges became competitors to the university, rather than collaborators.

As the war began, the university continued to establish its own student institutions, particularly in the wake of the transfer of the Manitoba College students to the university and the establishment of the arts faculty. The first intra-university sporting contest, a track meet with the University of North Dakota, was held in September 1914 on the Winnipeg Exhibition Grounds. The university student body began the publication of a semi-monthly journal, called *The Manitoban,* on 5 November 1914. A few weeks later, the University Dramatic Society held its first University Theatre Night at the Walker Theatre. It presented Bjornson's *The Bankrupt,* under the direction of Mrs. C.P. Walker. The university orchestra played for the occasion, as well. A few weeks later still, the first international debate between the University of Manitoba and the University of North Dakota was held, with 500 people in attendance.

As for St. John's College, its college council did not immediately respond to these substantial changes with any discussion or revisions of existing policy. The college was apparently still happy with the position it had formulated in 1907–08. Student enrolment in 1913–14 showed:

	MALES	FEMALES
Arts 1	13	5
Arts 2	10	4
3rd Year	6	6
4th Year	5	1
Total	**34**	**16**

Of these fifty students, twelve had addresses outside Winnipeg, and two resided out of the province (in Saskatchewan). The first college response to university teaching in arts and sciences came in May 1915, when the college council approved a new three-year course in theology, with arts subjects added, "for Students not looking to Matriculation in the University." The theology faculty, at least in part, would operate independently of the university.

At the beginning of the Great War, the main campus of the University of Manitoba was still downtown on Broadway, with each of the colleges and the medical school established on its own site somewhere else. Only St. Boniface College and St. John's College were far removed physically from Broadway, however. From 1911 onward, a terrace on University Place had been rented for the departments of history, political economy, and English. In 1915 the government allowed the university temporary use of parts of several other buildings, including the east wing of the former Deaf and Dumb Institute and the south wing of the old courthouse. With the location pendulum swinging back to downtown, the St. John's College council in April 1915 struck a committee to consider the construction of a college building on its site on Osborne Street. This council meeting was attended by professors Coombes, Murray, and Matheson, the first time that faculty had sat on council. This important change came without any motion noted in the minutes. A subsequent May meeting requested a financial report on the funding for the Osborne Street building, particularly Canon Garton's fundraising, and it was reported in October 1915 that the college fund raised by Garton involved $69,501.58 in pledges, $42,010.22 that had been paid, and $10,005.97 that "had been defrayed in Expenses—Salary, house-rent, travelling &c—from 1904–1913."

One of the first overt signs of the war on the university campus was the organization in November 1914 of a University Belgian Relief Fund, which raised $116.75 at St. John's College. By December 1914, however, the college magazine published a list of "St. John's Volunteers," consisting of forty past and present Johnians who were already serving in the Canadian armed forces. The magazine subsequently wrestled with the questions of the position to be taken by theological and non-theological students regarding the war. While it pointed out the complications of divided duty for the theological student, the magazine saw no such problems for the ordinary student. It urged every male student who was physically capable to "hasten to serve his country actively in her hour of need." Shortly thereafter, the editorialist was himself called to report at Montreal for immediate training. The April 1915 issue of the magazine commented on the earlier formation of the St. John's College Company of the University of Manitoba Contingent Canadian Officers' Training Corps. The report complained that St. John's Company was not doing its bit. Out of a student enrolment of seventy, only twenty-eight had attended twenty parades, and only eleven had "made themselves efficient by doing 40 drills." The next issue noted that the Rev. Canon E.E.M. Phair had died in the sinking of the ocean liner *Lusitania* by a German submarine. That same June 1915 issue printed a "roll of honor" consisting of thirty-nine names in the first contingent of St. John's volunteers, twenty-five in the second contingent, and ten names in the third contingent. The war doubtless affected the numbers of students in the graduating class of 1915, which consisted of seven women and only three men. The college magazine's report on the graduating class of 1915 made special mention of Joseph Cherniack, "a son of Judah hailing from Russia," who not only graduated from St. John's but brought several of his compatriots to the college. During his final year, Cherniak read a paper on "Zionism" to the St. John's College Literary Society. The college's location in the North End doubtless contributed to the intake of Jewish students.

In its October 1915 issue, the college magazine reported on smaller numbers, noting that "twenty-two of our boys, in all, have joined direct from the College." The roll of honour in that issue of former students and Old Boys stood at a full 130 names and continued subsequently to grow. By 1916 college enrolment was in serious trouble. The warden announced at the council meeting of 24 February 1916 "that the majority of the students were enlisting & that the College would be seriously depleted next year." Shortly thereafter, he died, and was not immediately replaced. The college magazine added in its April 1916 issue that "there is a mere handful of students remaining in residence, not one of whom, we are confident, but would join the colors at once did not some barrier stand in his way." By this time the roll of honour stretched to four full pages, and the magazine was beginning to publish accounts of fatalities on the battlefield. The August 1918 issue of the magazine would offer accounts of the deaths of thirty-one soldiers who had been associated with St. John's College and the college school. Distinctions and decorations included two CMGs, one VC, four DSOs, one DSC, twenty-four MCs, one DFC, two Croix de Guerre, three DCMs, three MMs, five "mentioned in Despatches," and one Order of St. John of Jerusalem (to Mrs. William M. Gordon, a nurse). The total number of deaths on the college honour roll in the 1918–19 calendar totalled forty-eight. St. John's College deaths and decorations were well beyond the college's proportion of students within the university. The 1918–19 yearbook noted with pride that university members had won one VC, two CMGs, two Officer of the Order of the British Empire awards, twelve DSOs, sixty military crosses, a Distinguished Flying Cross, and twenty military medals. With sadness it reported that 120 members of the university community had been killed in action or had died in active service.

Enrolment was affected not only by the war, of course, but by the growth of the university. As some had feared, the university arts courses were obviously depleting the numbers of students at St. John's College. The enrolment figures for the wartime period show a steady decline after the 1914–15 year in both male and female students enrolled in arts; there were no college students enrolled in science or engineering: The drop-off in male students was perhaps explicable in terms of the war, but one wonders how the college administration explained the loss of female students:

1913–14, 50 students (16 females)

1914–15, 65 students (14 females)

1915–16, 29 students (4 females)

1916–17, 10 students (3 females, plus 8 in special theology, all males)

1917–18, 11 students (2 females, plus 3 in special theology, all males)

1918–19, 14 students (2 females)

Also in trouble were college finances and fundraising. The college council had tried to encourage a Lenten appeal for the college by sending a statement to each clergyman in the diocese showing the tuitions remissions to boys and theological students, but Bishop Grisdale spoke "feelingly" to the council meeting of 31 October 1916 of the "inadequate response to the appeal for the new college," despite the fact that the appeal was being couched as a memorial for Archbishop Machray. That same meeting discussed the assumption of college control over Rupert's Land Ladies College, the female equivalent of the college school. The takeover was approved a month later and completed early in 1917. The college assumed the present mortgage of $24,250 and interest of $1800, as well as $4300 in taxes and $3800 of indebtedness in return for all the Rupert's Land Ladies College property, both real and personal. It agreed to carry on the school as a boarding and day school from year to year, with the understanding that it could close the school at any point where expenditure considerably exceeded revenue. Why the college took this action, particularly given its own situation, is not revealed in the council minutes.

In 1917 the province finally accepted financial responsibility for the university it had brought into existence some forty years earlier. Professor Chester Martin reported in the 1916–17 yearbook with obvious pleasure that the University of Manitoba had become a proper "Provincial Institution." Not all members of the university community, especially those in the colleges, were equally certain that the university's successes were necessarily a good thing, however. In 1917 the provincial government, at the request of the university council, amended the University Act to replace the old university council (which had grown to seventy members and was quite unwieldy) with a board of governors of nine persons appointed by the lieutenant-governor in council (i.e., the cabinet). The board of governors had substantial powers of management and control of the university and its policy. The university council was retained with smaller numbers as the academic wing, responsible for such matters as examinations and degree granting, admissions requirements, and the regulation of the standing of students, but not for policy.

Departmental and faculty business passed through the council to the board, which was ultimately responsible for everything. A subsequent amendment made the government responsible for the finances of the university, which had very few financial resources of its own. University assets consisted of $100,000 in buildings; a land endowment fund of $802,000, which yielded $37,000 income in 1917; unsold land from endowment of 52,363 acres; and the Isbister bequest of $125,000, which yielded $5850 per annum. The university was using old surplus government buildings, mainly downtown. The 1917 legislation left the colleges in affiliation and with rights to teach, but they had no representation on the board of governors. The denominational schools no longer had any power over the university. Instead, control had been vested in a small group of businessmen drawn from the traditional elite of the province, and especially the city of Winnipeg. The separation of financial from academic administration was total and quite distinctive to Manitoba. Few other places had businessmen as confident that they knew best how to run academic institutions. The president of the university would not become chief executive officer of the university until 1921, and always felt his hands were tied by the board.

Also in 1917, an agreement was made between Rupert's Land Ladies College Ltd. (RLLC) and St. John's College, by which RLLC transferred its property real and personal to St. John's College, in return for which the college assumed the mortgage indebtedness of the ladies college, taxes, and current liabilities. The RLLC claimed that "the War and business conditions generally have resulted in a material decrease of attendance of pupils and consequently a serious falling off of revenue." It would replace the moribund St. John's Ladies' College School and be operated as the female equivalent of St. John's College School until 1930. Like RLLC, St. John's College emerged from the Great War with its student body badly depleted, its raison d'être uncertain, and its internal leadership virtually non-existent. Although it would recover somewhat during the 1920s and early 1930s, the college would be struck an almost fatal blow in 1932, when an audit revealed that its unpaid bursar, also the chief financial officer for the Anglican diocese of Rupert's Land and for the university, had been systematically embezzling from the funds under his direction for many years. Enrolment in the college (as distinct from the various college schools) recovered slowly from the various blows of the war. In 1918–19 twelve students from St. John's College were enrolled in first-year arts at the university, three in second-year, and none in third- and fourth-year courses. By 1921–22 there were fifteen first-years, thirteen second-years, six third-years, and two fourth-years, for a grand total of thirty-six; few of them were females. Other sources place the total St. John's College numbers at this time at fifty, which means there were fifteen theological students not taking university courses. In his published memoir, Warden G.A. Wells wrote that the fifteen theology students included five returned soldiers with some training in England and two Irishmen with no training whatever. Not only were enrolment figures low, but the percentage of students from the university who did considerable work in the college was miniscule. In 1923–24, only twenty-four of 1182 arts students in the university did all their training at St. John's, and another twelve were part-timers.

A number of decisions by the warden-less college council in 1919 and 1920 suggest that at best that body in these years immediately after the war had a policy for the college of marking time. More likely, the unspoken policy was really one of concentration on Anglican secondary education in the Ladies' College School and the college school. In 1919 the Ladies Advisory

Committee of Rupert's Land Ladies College, consisting of a number of the city's most prominent matrons, including Mrs. E.L. Drewrey and Lady Nanton, was confirmed by college council as the executive committee of management for the ladies' college. The same meeting of the council considered an offer to buy the unoccupied Osborne Street lot for $50,000, and awarded the potential purchaser a first refusal. The deal fell through, but a series of resolutions in early 1920 showed that although the council did not believe that the university would move from its present site for many years, it also believed the college should remain at its present site rather than moving to the downtown Osborne location.

To some extent the decision not to move downtown was a consequence of the inability to create enthusiasm for fundraising in the Anglican community. In 1919 the alumni of the college had proposed a "Forward Movement" campaign to raise $300,000 for the college and its schools. This target would include $70,000 for Rupert's Land Ladies College, $30,000 for the warden's endowment, and $200,000 for a new building and equipment for the school.* This proposal was shelved later in deference to the "Church Forward" campaign of the diocese and because of "the difficulty of raising money required at the present time." The college council decided, however, to inform the alumni of the pressing needs of the college school in the hopes that money would be donated for the purpose. One of the reasons for appointing G.A. Wells as warden in 1921 was because he was a prominent Old Boy of the college school and an alumnus of the college. Wells was counted on to be useful in fundraising.

Unable to attract sufficient attendance for major decisions at meetings in the summer of 1919, the council settled that year for making repairs and additions to the school building that were "absolutely necessary." Full tenders for a proposed new wing and gymnasium for the school were thus not entertained until March 1920. The finance committee (chaired by John

---

* The records also included an entry of $10,000 for country land for the school, but to add this amount to the others would make $310,000.

A. Machray) reported in April that before proceeding with construction, at least $50,000 of the money required should be secured by subscription in cash collected as a result of a crash campaign targeted at alumni, parents, and interested churchmen. It also wanted the architect's plans revised so that the new addition "might be transformed into an Apartment Block whenever the time comes for selling it." That time would come when a new college building needed to be built near whatever site was eventually chosen for the university. The 1920 crash campaign met with some success from the Old Boys, but with little response in the city "owing to business conditions." The college council ended up requesting that half the proceeds of the diocesan "Forward Movement" campaign be allocated to the college for the college school, a request unlikely to be fulfilled. The plans for the building were subsequently scaled down and much of the construction ultimately financed with a loan from Sun Life and Great West Life Assurance Societies. Despite the inability to pay cash for the construction of the building, Archbishop Samuel Matheson, acting as chancellor, reluctantly agreed to proceed. The new addition would be called Hamber Hall after a wealthy Old Boy living in Vancouver who had donated $30,000 towards its erection. According to the memoir of incoming Warden Wells, the artificial prosperity at the end of the war led parents to think that they had the additional funds to support a son in boarding school. When the boom quickly collapsed, the decision to add increased residential space for the school proved to be an expensive mistake.

In 1921 the college negotiated with the diocese an agreement providing funds for the endowment of a warden's chair, provided the money could be collected from the parishes. As a result, a meeting of college council on 14 September 1921 introduced to council the Reverend (Lt. Col.) George Anderson Wells, CMG, the newly appointed warden of the college. Wells (1877–1964) had been born in Newfoundland, served in the Boer War as a volunteer at the eventual rank of sergeant, and had attended the college school and college as a mature student between 1904 and 1910. He had actually spent two years gaining his senior matriculation, studying with college school students half his age. He had subsequently worked for one year (1909–10) as editor of the *St. John's College Magazine,* and for two years had been president of the University of Manitoba Debating Union. Wells had then served with distinction as a senior chaplain during the Great War and been decorated.

The new warden was in many respects a perfect choice: an old Johnian, a decorated war veteran, and a former Anglican chaplain to boot. He was also a bluff no-nonsense man, with few intellectual pretensions, who believed in getting things done. He had only just accepted a parish appointment at St. Margaret's, Winnipeg, a few months earlier when he was invited to take on the college leadership. Some controversy developed over the process of the appointment. Nominated by a committee of council chaired by John A. Machray, Wells's appointment was announced in the newspapers before the council had formally ratified his nomination. The premature announcement was blamed on an overzealous reporter. The council voted him an annual salary of $3500 and a house. It also noted that the duties of the warden, especially with relation to the college school, needed to be defined more clearly. This, as it turned out, proved to be an understatement. A committee subsequently reported that, for the time being, the warden of the college should also serve as headmaster of the school. Since the dean of the college had been in impaired health since September 1921, the warden ended up also serving as acting dean until 1922. In 1921 the *St. John's College Magazine* changed its name to *The Johnian,* and became less academically serious for the period of the 1920s. Traditional features such as "Exchanges" (excerpts from fellow publications), "Alumni Notes," and "Notes on Activities" were maintained, and a larger number of jokes made their appearance.

The first major policy decision made by the new warden regarding the college came before the college council at its April 1922 meeting. It involved coeducation. The role of women at the college had been problematic since their first admission. Numbers had remained small and enrolments had fallen off to almost nil at the end of the war. Wells approached the question of female students obliquely, noting the need for increased accommodations for male students and "also for a suitable residence for women students." If a women's residence could not be provided, he recommended that no women be admitted for the next academic year. A lively discussion ensued. The council agreed that accommodation should not be increased by new building. It authorized the warden to look into rental of a suitable house for a women's residence, and refused to admit girls who had not matriculated. At this point the college had virtually no female students remaining in attendance. Perhaps this situation was partially a result of the lack of a women's residence, although a variety of limitations, formal and informal, on female students no doubt led them to prefer to register directly at the university. In any event, an ensuing meeting heard that the only suitable house available for female students was presently occupied by junior boys. The house could accommodate twenty boys, and obviously could not be used for students of both sexes. The income from that number of boarders would be about $1800 per annum. The council decided "that it would not be wise to take this house from the School," thus continuing the policy begun after the war of preferring the school over the college and moving closer to a decision that no female students would be admitted. A council meeting in May 1922 heard an offer from Canon Matheson to use his house for female students, providing a smaller suitable house could be secured for him. Apparently nothing could be worked out on this front, and at a council meeting on 5 September 1922 the warden reported that the situation regarding a residence for female students remained unchanged. The council decided that a permanent policy would be made at a subsequent meeting. In the meantime, no further female students were admitted to St. John's College throughout the period of the 1920s, thus producing yet another incarnation for the institution in the form of a return to an all-male student body.

Chapter Six

An All-Male College and a Return to Coeducation, 1923–1932

THE PERIOD OF THE 1920S AND EARLY 1930S—the two can be seen as one because the Great Depression had very little immediate effect on St. John's College—were, in general, years of great financial uncertainty and instability for the college and its schools. A prevailing sense of unfocussed unhappiness with the direction of finances and financial management characterized this period, but nobody ever really managed to identify the problem. Warden Wells came close on several occasions, but never succeeded in making the breakthrough, or, at least, backed away from it. As a result, the college scuffled around with various strategies for making ends meet, none of which seemed quite to work.

Up until the beginning of the Depression, both Winnipeg and Manitoba shared in the experience of the uneven economic prosperity characteristic of much of the 1920s. Drought and reduced international demand for grain both cut substantially into farm incomes, and the foreign sales of mineral resources were totally flat. Manitobans joined other Canadians in various speculative activities that could produce huge windfall gains. Historian James Gray characterized the era as "The Gambling Decade," pointing out that it was characterized by veering off in new directions and risking for the sake of risk. Winnipeggers "shot the works" on the football pools, at the racetrack, on grain futures at the Grain Exchange, and on oil and gas futures on the stock exchange. Like St. John's College itself, Manitoba society—still dominated by British-born Protestants who prided themselves on their secure place in the British Empire—had some vague misgivings that all was not well, but could not quite identify the problem.

In 1923 Warden Wells introduced for the arts program a two-year course in religious education. To provide a core of students, he insisted that the course be compulsory for theology students. But the success of the course required arts enrolments. Wells hoped it would attract prospective teachers. The course covered the history and philosophy of education and educational psychology. It was never particularly popular with either theology students or arts students, although its presence led to a constant search during the 1920s for money to endow a chair of religious education.

According to his memoirs, from the beginning of his appointment Warden Wells was troubled about the finances of the college. The various bursaries, many of which had been raised by Archbishop Machray, were administered by the treasurer of the diocese (John Machray), who informed Wells what monies were available but not where the money had originated. Wells sought to raise additional endowments for bursaries for theological students. He obtained funds for a Soldiers' Memorial Bursary, mainly from Old Boys who had served. He solicited ex-students of Canon Phair for funds as a memorial to him, and got Lady Schultz to put up $5000 in memory of her husband. Wells later claimed that he had the good sense to insist that all bursary recipients sign a declaration that he would spend at least one year in the diocese after ordination. If the recipient did not do so, he was to return the money in instalments. This policy actually returned some money from the bursaries. Wells also claimed that he had insisted that any donations made to him be converted by the college's investment agents, Machray and Sharpe, into registered bonds in the name of the warden of the college. He also insisted on being shown the actual bonds.* The money raised was in 1924 duly invested in Manitoba 5 percent bonds, due in 1943 and registered to the warden. The immediate problem with the bursaries was not with Machray and Sharpe, but with the archbishop, who insisted that Wells's fundraising was competing with the other campaigns of the college. Wells argued that none of the money he had raised would have been given to other projects.

Wells and Archbishop Matheson clashed directly late in 1922 over finances, particularly the debt for the construction of Hamber Hall, which had not yet been extinguished. Lurking behind the conflict was considerable confusion over the administrative roles of the chancellor (Matheson) and the warden (Wells). The archbishop wrote the warden a letter, in which he maintained that Wells, whom he described as executive officer of the council, was the individual "to put machinery into play to carry out its obligations." More specifically, the archbishop wanted Wells to take the lead in canvassing laymen and Old Boys in the city in order to retire the building debt, rather than going about raising small amounts for theological bursaries. Matheson was also convinced that Wells should have been doing more in the diocese to publicize the college, so that contributions toward his salary voted by synod would be forthcoming. He offered his remarks as guidance only, he wrote.

Wells replied that fundraising to retire the building debt should not be undertaken until the financial position of the college school was clear. This would involve a full financial report, on which an auditor was still working. Obviously transparency over the funds of both the school and the college was already an ongoing problem, and Wells on his own testimony would take the lead in attempting to get the books properly audited. At this task he was not, as we shall see, very successful. The warden further insisted that not he but the archbishop as chancellor was the executive officer of the

---

* In the long run this ploy would not succeed in saving the bonds, which apparently were illegally converted into cash some time before the defalcation.

college council. He added that he would not have accepted the appointment as warden had he understood that it was his job to raise either his own salary or to pay off back debts incurred by the college school. Warden Wells was a blunt, outspoken man, and he not surprisingly concluded his letter by objecting to the archbishop's not very subtle attempts at guidance, writing, "please do not treat me as a child. I have worked among MEN and have led where men were needed." Wells subsequently told college council that he wished his only connection with the college school to be the provision of daily services in the chapel and the preparation of boys for confirmation, and he hoped an ordained priest would be added to the school staff to handle these matters as soon as possible.

Financial problems arose again in December 1922. An audit of the books and accounts of the college and the college school was presented to the college council. This audit grew out of a general sense that the finances of the college were not properly understood by the council, although no one had any clear idea what the problem might be. The immediate result of the audit was to show an operating deficit. The committee reporting on the audit (of which John Machray was a member) noted that no conclusions could be drawn about the financial state of the college "until the set of books has opened for the Bursar showing all capital assets and Liabilities of the Corporation, together with revenue and expenditure in connection therewith." The report continued, "The college has received revenue from some endowment sources, while the general endowment has been depleted to maintain Real Estate assets. While endowment revenue is taken into account in the operating statement the loss in general endowment does not appear." Moreover, added the committee, although much money had been spent on the school and raised for the school, "the school has no assets: all assets being vested in the College." This was the first occasion that anybody in authority had suggested that the school was being held in thrall to the college, rather than the reverse. Furthermore, the school charged $452 per annum for tuition and board, while the scale elsewhere at Canadian Anglican and private schools was as follows: Ridley, $700; Trinity College School, $650; Bishop's College School, $750; Appleby

Oakville, $750; St. Andrew's, Toronto, $750. The committee recommended that the bursar open a set of books showing all capital assets and liabilities of the corporation, and that this be reconciled with the administrator's books, and that an inventory of assets for college and school be taken.

As a result of this discussion, a motion to proceed with an audit of the capital account was adopted. A report on the audit of the capital account was made by the chairman of the finance committee, John Machray. This lengthy report did not actually include an audited statement of the trust accounts, but rather went on about operating procedures, arguing that the average charge of seven dollars for board and lodging barely covered actual costs, with no money left for interest, taxes, and depreciation. Fees must be raised, it insisted (boarding fees were subsequently increased to $8.50 per week). In the end the report recommended separate boards of management for the school and the college. The report covered financial matters only up to 31 December 1921. It recommended that the bursar submit to the college council semi-annual statements of the trust funds, and that a separate bank account be kept for each trust fund and the monies deposited therein (obviously dealing with income rather than the trust money itself). The committee noted that unimproved real estate, mostly on Main Street, was worth $129,930. This should be sold, it said. An adjustment of trust funds could be done after the audit was complete to 31 July 1923. Warden Wells later recollected, "Now and then a small financial committee or sub-committee of the Council would be appointed to investigate our finances but nothing further was heard of their findings. Perhaps I thought this a bit off, but like the rest of [the members of college council] I was confident there was a reasonable explanation." The audit to be completed to 31 July 1923 remained unsubmitted in December 1923, and the council requested from John Machray that a full report be forwarded not later than 31 December 1923. This deadline was not met.

A separate report at this time dealt with the professoriate endowment, which was vested in a trust deed between the Bishop of Rupert's Land and the college dated 1886. This report was not concerned with an audit, but was simply a statement of policy regarding the use of the endowment solely to pay professorial salaries. Some funds had been taken from the professoriate fund to pay back taxes, chiefly on unimproved Main Street property, and a motion was made that the money be restored. At council there was continual evidence of financial disarray and staffing problems. At a council meeting in March 1923, Warden Wells raised the question of the source of salary for the new lecturer in church music. A committee was appointed to look into the matter of the trusteeship of the professoriate funds of unoccupied chairs. Council in May 1923 was told by the warden of the uncertain situation within the various theological chairs and the desperate need for full-time appointments. That same meeting voted to appoint Mr. Thomas Boon to take full charge of the stewardship of the college. Boon, who had been associated with the college on a part-time basis since 1921, thus began a long full-time involvement. The college council also voted to continue the committee for Rupert's Land Ladies College. As part of Warden Wells's campaign for additional funding, in 1923 the diocesan women's auxiliary provided a studentship of $400 per year for training of a missionary for work among First Peoples. The same organization also gave money for new gowns for the theological students. The matter of the warden's chair endowment continued unsettled into 1923. The library was the recipient of a small annual grant of $150 from the college council to buy "up-to-date reference books."

The college still had not attempted to address the question of its role or its future. Some forward thinking was provided externally. In June 1923 a commission to examine the educational facilities of the province was appointed by the government, chaired by Walter Murray, president of the University of Saskatchewan. The commission hired Dr. W.S. Learned, the assistant secretary of the Carnegie Foundation for the Advancement of Teaching, to study the university and the agricultural college. Learned did not much like the Guelph model of an independent agricultural college, and recommended against it. More to the point for St. John's College, he also noted that "the part played by the colleges in the life of the present University is relatively insignificant" and recommended that the church colleges should be relocated on the new university campus to provide a proper "moral purpose" to intellectual affairs and to provide unity in citizenship and principle. The colleges, wrote Learned, could "maintain for [their] students an environment that fosters clean living, intimate and wholesale associations, and the growth of an intelligent and convincing moral purpose in intellectual affairs." He opposed the union of Manitoba and Wesley colleges, preferring instead "for each to retain its identity and develop as a separate unit." Learned wanted the new colleges to develop with professors "who take a somewhat broader view of their responsibilities to their students than does the average university professor." Thus he wanted each college to maintain "on its own foundation a small group of recognized University teachers." He saw the need for certain "common standards of training, status, salary, and so forth, in collegiate faculties." He even saw that the university might well advise in which college departments appointments should be made, but agreed they should remain collegiate appointments. Learned was influenced both by the English model for colleges and by the American liberal arts college, both of which he sought imaginatively to combine with the growing multi-university that was the University of Manitoba.

For the moment nothing was done about Dr. Learned's report, which was never discussed in college council. Instead, money (or its absence) continued to be on everyone's minds. In his memoirs, Warden Wells wrote that he actually had some evidence in the fall of 1923 of the seriousness of the financial problem. At a dinner in Brandon, a former member of the office of the auditor who was watchdog of the financial affairs of John Machray's firm asserted that "in all the years he was connected with the college in the capacity of auditor, there was never a proper audit made." Wells challenged this remark, and was told that audits of the books had never involved an actual examination of the securities themselves. Wells returned to Winnipeg to confront Archbishop Matheson about these charges. Matheson replied that he had in his safe the synod journals with properly certified auditor's statements. Wells replied that these audits probably did not include the securities, and Matheson discovered that this was indeed the case. Matheson promised to investigate, but never did. Wells added that when the diocese of Brandon was separated from Rupert's Land in 1924, he had proposed that the college trust funds be handed over to the treasurer of the Rupert's Land synod, who now had far less work to do than before. Archbishop Matheson replied that "our present machinery is quite safe and adequate for conducting the financial affairs of the college." Wells wrote in his memoirs, "I am on record as having tried to do something," but his manoeuvring then (and later) always stopped short of actually blowing the whistle. John Machray teetered on a knife-edge for many years, but nobody actually came forward before 1932 to insist on a proper audit of the trust funds in his charge. College council kept voting that the committee report on the audit at the next meeting, but this never quite happened and whatever financial reports were made did not involve the actual securities. In fairness to Warden Wells, he and the archbishop had never seen eye to eye on financial matters. To bring to a head a situation involving Matheson's beloved protegé, John Machray, would risk ending a career.

One major reason why the endowment fund securities did not get properly audited and examined was because the college throughout the 1920s continued to operate at a regular deficit. This meant that most attention to financial matters was devoted to immediate crisis management rather than to what seemed longer-term problems. John Machray seems to have encouraged a concentration on operating expenses. Something called an auditor's balance sheet through 31 July 1923 finally appeared at a council meeting on 9 June 1924 in a finance committee's report, which did not deal with securities at all, but pointed out that much of the 1923–24 revenue (over $10,000 worth) was employed liquidating 1922–23 past-due accounts. The college desperately needed to liquidate floating indebtedness, reported the bursar, and if it could do so, could operate at a small surplus. The bursar suggested the usual remedies: increases in fees, increases in attendance and residence, sale of vacant land, donations, and special appeals, adding that small fee increases were already in place and insisting that selling land and raising money through special appeals were dubious options at best. At this same meeting, the special committee on the audit noted that it was not in a position to comment on the auditor's report on the capital account, adding: "as you know, the various funds in various trusts are well and carefully invested and the situation of the various trusts would seem to be in good order, although it is possible that there may be a shrinkage in assets represented by vacant real estate if a revision in valuation were made."

Rupert's Land Ladies College, of which John Machray was chancellor, appeared to be doing better than before St. John's College had taken it over, and also better than the college itself. A financial statement showed a debit balance of $11.43, but both the archbishop and Mr. Machray insisted that the ladies' college actually had a credit balance. During the 1922–23 academic year, the ladies' college had enrolled 214 girls, fourteen of them in boarding. The deficit of the ladies' college had been regularly reduced out of earnings. Some members of the council may have wondered why the college itself could not do as well. Part of the answer was enrolment. According to the warden's report of 27 May 1925, in the 1924–25 academic year only sixty-eight students were enrolled in the college. Thirty-two were in theology, fifteen in first-year arts, and thirteen in second-year arts. Numbers had not risen appreciably since the war. Unasked questions about financial performance may have seemed to be answered at a council meeting on 23 October 1924, when John Machray—out of the blue, following yet another tedious discussion about money—offered "to act as Bursar for the ensuing year without salary." This offer was speedily accepted. The post was vacant because Walter Burman had been promoted to acting headmaster of the college school. The modern reader of the council minutes—blessed with hindsight—wants to take the council collectively by its suit lapels and shake it for allowing Machray to monopolize all signing and dispersing authority in his own hands, making it more difficult to audit him properly. But its members at the time had a quite different view. Machray was, after all, a financial wizard. The financial problems he would inherit were slowly accumulating, however. Among these were the back taxes owed by the college to the city of Winnipeg. When the amount was finally ascertained, it amounted to just under $15,000.

Another possible way of dealing with the financial crisis emerged briefly in 1925. The Learned report of 1923 finally bore some fruit in that year. Warden Wells had read the report with considerable interest and care, and in 1924 had corresponded with Dr. Learned about it. That year Wells had even broached the subject of the Carnegie Foundation's assisting the college in founding a chair for education. The Foundation's assistant secretary, W.S. Learned, had, after all, done the report for the province on higher education in 1923. Nothing had come of this initiative, but John Mackay of Manitoba College had also contacted Learned, and was told that his 1923 report "was made with the idea of establishing something like the Oxford system in Manitoba." In March 1925 Mackay had taken the lead in organizing a consortium of colleges, backed by the university and the province, to apply to the Carnegie Foundation for money. Unfortunately, the initiative was not based on very much discussion and planning. It was all too transparently a desperate search for external funding rather than a sincere attempt to fulfill a well-articulated vision.

The possibility of external funds certainly galvanized St. John's College into preparing a brief statement of its present position and needs. The statement described St. John's College as an institution with university-level students in arts and theology and with two matriculation schools, one for boys and one for girls. The schools could feed the college "when we are in a position to accommodate those who come to us." The statement emphasized that the college was not adequately serving the Church of England constituency attending the university, but it did not attempt to explain why this was so. The college required salary increases for staff and an additional lectureship in religious education. It also needed money to move into closer touch with the university at whatever its final site would be. The college thus needed endowment providing an income of $13,000 a year for teaching (about $250,000 in total) and the sum of $300,000 for new buildings. A covering letter from Chancellor Matheson elaborated the

St. John's "ideal" as he saw it. It was nothing new. The colleges would do the bulk of the teaching of the university in the first two years. The restriction to first- and second-year courses would relieve the colleges of the expense of hiring specialists, who should be provided by the "State University." The entire tone of the application was one of a cap-in-hand request by poor Canadian neighbours.

At a St. John's College council meeting on 12 June 1925, Warden Wells proudly announced that three of the denominational colleges (Manitoba, Wesley, and St. John's) at the University of Manitoba, with the approval of the university president and the premier, had applied to the Carnegie Foundation for the Advancement of Teaching for a $1-million grant to develop the colleges in a manner "similar to that in the Colleges of Oxford and Cambridge." This phrase, it should be emphasized, was used in private correspondence and in the minutes of the council rather than in the actual application to the foundation. The application itself spoke of financial assistance to enable the colleges to increase their professorial staff and enable them to do research and supervise post-graduate work, as well as providing for tutors recruited from the post-graduates to deal with much of the undergraduate teaching.

A conference was held in New York on 18 June to discuss the matter with Dr. Keppell of the Carnegie Corporation. The college had voted to send the warden and Mr. J.A. Machray as its representatives. The council was obviously more than a bit skeptical of the whole business. Wells and Machray were to pay their own expenses, which would be reimbursed only if the application were successful. In the end, Machray did not attend. Those at the conference were not encouraged by the Carnegie people. The Carnegie Foundation had already made a $3-million commitment to the Maritime provinces and could not make another large grant to the Winnipeg colleges, the people from Winnipeg were told. Carnegie might make some small grants "to help along the situation," but only of a sort that would not lead the Winnipeg institutions to "capitalize such grants in their minds." Walter Riddell of Wesley College got the corporation to agree to consider a modest grant in the autumn, but only in competition with other applications for money from the special fund. A subsequent letter from the colleges to the fund asking for $36,000 per year over five years proved that the Manitoba educators had not really listened to what the Carnegie people had said about modest amounts. This letter produced a reply that as "this Foundation has no funds for such purposes as that which you suggest," it assumed that the request was intended for the Carnegie Corporation itself and thus forwarded the letter there. Warden Wells did not give up. He wrote the foundation in 1926, asking for some small assistance for the lectureship in religious education, but was rejected on the grounds of lack of funds. The Carnegie card was played out for the moment, although it would serendipitously return again in 1932.

On 2 July 1925, Warden Wells reported to the council on his trip to New York City. The council did the only thing possible. It voted to thank the Carnegie Foundation for its "courteous and sympathetic hearing," and returned to the monotonous business of discussing "what steps can be taken to deal with the financial condition of the College and School." A few days later, Bursar Machray was authorized to appeal to the "friends of the college" for financial assistance in reducing the debt. Machray succeeded in collecting $1500. In his report for 1925, Steward Thomas Boon recorded the unpaid taxes at $8377. He also noted that the educational side of the college and school were in surplus by $9237, but the residential side had lost $7453. Boon added that "steady and continuous pressure" on outstanding accounts had brought in $4400 and the amount still owing was fairly small. Early in 1926 Bursar Machray recommended consolidating the mortgage and back taxes and paying them off with a loan. He also announced that he had a tentative offer for the Osborne Street property of $60,000. The sale of this property would drag on for years. Enrolment for 1925–26 was up. It stood as seventy-eight in the college (forty in residence), and 237 in the school (eighty-eight in residence). However, the college total included fourteen third- and fourth-year arts students, twenty-two matriculation students, and eight special theology students. There were fifteen students in first-year arts, and nineteen in second-year arts. This was the highest number since 1921–22. After 1925 and until 1930, the college taught arts subjects and chemistry only in the first and second year, and offered only a limited number of courses (philosophy, Hellenistic Greek, religious education) for third- and fourth-year students.

Despite occasional promising signs, Warden Wells reported in March 1927 that the annual loss on administration had reached $6000 for the year just ended. According to Steward Boon, further economies in operation were virtually impossible and operating costs for old buildings could only increase. "What we need," he wrote in his report, "is new money which can be invested to produce revenue, or to discharge the obligations on which we now have to pay interest." The warden recommended resolving the immediate financial problem by dropping modern languages and closing the junior house. A committee appointed to deal with economy rejected Wells's recommendations. It suggested instead a number of small savings, the largest of which was in the number of people employed to maintain the buildings and grounds and to run the kitchens. The savings included not printing a new college calendar, reducing the library budget to $100, and shutting down the college telephone as soon as examinations were over. Wells continued to be uneasy about the overall financial situation, and, after examining the books of the general endowment fund, wrote the chancellor a letter dated 18 May 1927 about the depletion of that fund for taxes and "other things" to the amount of over $30,000 between 1916 and 1925. Archbishop Matheson replied, agreeing to discuss "the depletion of the capital of the General Endowment Fund" as soon as possible. But according to Wells in his memoir, nothing was ever done. There was certainly no report of any discussion in the council minutes. A council meeting in June 1927, instead of discussing the endowment fund, decided to borrow money "to clean up the Steward's indebtedness."

The financial situation improved for the next several years. St. John's College was unexpectedly aided in 1928 when the profits of military canteens operated during the war were distributed by the federal government. Manitoba got $200,000. Warden Wells was one of the three trustees of the canteen fund in the province. The trustees rejected a per capita distribution to veterans of the money, and instead agreed to pay the tuition fees of veterans and of the children of those who had died in battle. As Wells noted, St. John's College "had more veterans and fatherless children than all the other Faculties combined." Wells not only had scholarship money from the canteen fund, but, according to alumni, he allowed students to enrol without actually paying their fees. Finances began deteriorating again with the onset of the stock market crash late in 1929. In November of that year another commission appointed by the government reported on the site question. It had held extensive hearings on the matter. St. John's College had argued that the university should remain on Broadway, as had several other of the colleges. Despite much support for the Broadway site, the commission recommended that the university build at the agricultural college site and that the senior years of university instruction be moved there. The government accepted this recommendation and the site question was apparently finally resolved.

Despite the Depression and a steward's report in October 1930 that last year "was most disappointing and the outlook for this year not hopeful," the prospects for the college actually appeared relatively bright as the thirties began. Conditions for the ladies' school were not so rosy, and it quietly folded in 1930. A legislative act in March 1932 repealed the act of incorporation of St. John's College Ladies' School in 1932, vesting all assets (a $21,500 capital account of war bonds held by Machray & Sharpe) in the archbishop of Rupert's Land to provide annual grants for the college. As for the college, by April 1930 it had raised $47,154 as an endowment for the salary of the warden, and another $25,000 for the creation of a lectureship in religious education. In the autumn of 1930, the college resumed teaching senior division courses, and in 1931 women were readmitted. The reappearance of female students represented the next major institutional change for the college as it shifted back to coeducational status. *The Johnian* greeted the change with pleasure. It pointed out that St. John's had enrolled over 100 female students since first admitting them in 1891. The ladies had always been interested in hockey, the magazine insisted, and a St. John's ladies' hockey team had at one time gone through three consecutive seasons without losing a game. On the other hand, Warden Wells told *The Manitoban*, "I am not so sure that co-education is having the beneficial effect upon either the male or female members of the University that its advocates claim it does. As far as I can see the girls are becoming too much like men and the men too much like women." Thanks partly to the female intake, enrolment for 1931 reached 106 students, including seventy-one first-years in arts and science. On 31 January 1931, Archbishop Matheson finally resigned as chancellor of the university and St. John's College. He was replaced in September of that year by the Right Reverend I.O. Stringer, formerly bishop of the Yukon.

In 1930, under the editorship of W.L. Morton, *The Johnian* acquired a black cover and temporarily became a serious literary magazine. The literary bent of *The Johnian* was not greeted with much enthusiasm by the student body. As a result, the St. John's student council in 1931 began another student publication called *The Tatler*. It was printed on one-sided single sheets of legal-sized paper by the cyclostyle process and cost twenty-five cents per year. The journal called for an improved college spirit, but demonstrated that student life was still alive and well. It reported that W.L. "Bill" Morton had brought the debating cup back to St. John's, was editing the *Manitoban*, and had been nominated by the college as the president of the University of Manitoba Students' Union. Its pages were full of the doings of the dramatic society, the hockey team (it had won the Varsity Senior Trophy for two years running), and the debating team. One debate at the college was on the topic, "Resolved that the modern girl will make as good a house-keeper as her mother did." The literary society heard from Canon Herklots reading his book, *The English Essay*. That same year, under the editorship of W.L. Morton's sister, Margaret Morton, *The Johnian* was reformed, printing fewer issues in a smaller size and becoming more responsible to the college council. The cover became yellow and the literary emphasis was less pronounced. Its January 1932 issue boasted that the college had "undoubtedly turned out more hockey players of professional calibre than any other one institution in

Canada." It listed Eddie Shore of the Boston Bruins, Red Dutton of the New York Americans, Tommy Cook of the Chicago Blackhawks, and Andy Blair of the Toronto Maple Leafs as recent alumni.

In January 1932, George Locke, the chief librarian of the Toronto Public Library, wrote to the college that $100,000 had been set aside some years ago by the Carnegie Corporation of New York for aid to college libraries within British dominions. He invited the college to apply for some of the money and he enclosed a form to be completed. Warden Wells replied that it was difficult to fill in the form. He observed that the college had full use of the university library. At the same time, he wrote, the decision recently announced by the university to move senior division students to the Fort Garry campus (then called the St. Vital campus) would mean greater demands on the college library, now housed in five rooms, until the college could move to the new campus. In a subsequent letter, Locke emphasized "that the grants will be made to Colleges which are prepared to make an effort to develop their libraries—and not merely to 'needy' colleges." The college never pursued the matter further, partly because of the financial disclosures of 1932.

The prospective move to St. Vital obviously also led Warden Wells to begin to think about moving the college to the new university site as soon as the economy improved. As he wrote to Mr. Locke, "We have been waiting for this move of the University for many years and have blamed some of our backwardness on that fact." The province was committed in principle from 1930 to providing land at Fort Garry for the colleges. Wells had been in touch with W.S. Learned of the Carnegie Foundation in November 1931 and was encouraged by his interest in the Manitoba problem. On Wells's initiative in 1932, architectural plans for a new building were duly prepared by C.W.U. Chivers of Winnipeg in anticipation of a fundraising drive. Wells specified

> a Building with Chapel, Dining-room, Common-room, Lecture-rooms, Library, etc., to accommodate 50 students in residence, 25 of whom to be Theological students. Dining-room to seat 150, Chapel to seat 200. A house

for the Warden and a house for Women. Total cost $250,000. Arrangement to [be] made for an extension to house 50 more students at a cost of $50,000. The building to be of Manitoba stone in keeping with the University scheme.

The warden wanted to house students at Fort Garry and teach a limited curriculum in junior and senior arts, as well as in theology. This construction was to be financed chiefly by the Carnegie Foundation ($150,000) and by sale of college buildings; only $20,000 was to be raised through a general appeal. This financing scheme suggested just how removed from reality Wells's thinking was. In October 1932, after the defalcation, he suggested that his earlier plans could be used as the basis for discussing the future of St. John's College.

In the short run, the university's move was also expected to increase enrolment at St. John's, as many North End students would find the new location too difficult to reach. On the other hand, by 1932 the general economic climate was beginning to falter. In April 1932 Mr. A.D. Baker, Prof. J.F. Cross, and Warden Wells all agreed on a voluntary reduction of one month's salary for the year. Economies were also effected for office and school staff. At the same time, school headmaster W.A. Burman asked for a reduction in school fees for the ensuing year. Curiously enough, however, college enrolment was still going up. For the 1932–33 academic year, there were fifty first-year students (forty-four of them new), and twenty-four second-years (twenty-four of them new), plus twenty-five theological and non-fee-paying students. Including the third- and fourth-year students, there were now 120 enrolled at the college, a higher number than had ever been achieved in the past.

Then suddenly, on 24 August 1932, on the eve of the new academic year, headlines in the Winnipeg newspapers screamed that John A. Machray— nephew of Archbishop Machray, honourary bursar of the university, chairman of the board of governors, chancellor of the diocese, chancellor and bursar of St. John's College—had been arrested and charged with embezzling large amounts of money from the diocese, the university, and the college.

The college would never be the same.

Chapter Seven

More Financial Trouble,
1932–1945

THE DAY OF RECKONING HAD FINALLY ARRIVED. Peter could be robbed to pay Paul for only so long. Eventually John Machray's house of cards, like that of hundreds of financially overextended Manitobans over the past few years, had to collapse. On a warm August day in 1932, the only college staff physically in Winnipeg were Registrar Thomas Boon and Warden George A. Wells. The warden was unexpectedly summoned by telephone to call in downtown on the Attorney General of the province, William Major, who had been appointed to the college council a few months earlier. After a short preliminary conversation, Major explained his concern: "a million dollars of the church's funds have been lost; another million given by the Rockefeller Foundation to the University is also gone. The office of Machray & Sharpe is locked, and John A. Machray will be arrested today. A statement will appear in the daily papers tomorrow." Wells went immediately from the Attorney General's office to the house of retired archbishop Samuel

Matheson to break the news as gently as possible. Matheson was crushed. Then the warden returned to the college to see what could be salvaged from what was obviously going to be a total wreck.

For the Anglican community of Winnipeg, the debacle was both a physical and a moral disaster. In many ways the moral devastation was worse. A pillar of society, a man who had been completely trusted, proved to be a total fraud. His failure brought everyone down. As historian Arthur Lower pointed out in his autobiography, *My First Seventy-Five Years*, the Machray business ended the Manitoba equivalent of the Family Compact in Upper Canada. The older families, associated with the Hudson's Bay Company and the Anglican Church, wrote Lower, had "held on in positions of influence long after the old [Red River] colony had been submerged in the growing province."

Unlike most people in Manitoba, George Wells was not completely astounded by the news of John Machray's financial chicanery. He had suspected something was amiss with Machray's management of college trust funds for years, although he had not appreciated the scope of the peculations. The story first broke in the Winnipeg newspapers on 24 August. The initial amounts mentioned were relatively small. Machray was charged in provincial court with theft of $47,451.37 in money and securities from the university, most of it from the Isbister scholarship fund. The amounts involved escalated daily. By 26 August, the *Tribune* headline read: "University Fund of $500,000 Reported Almost Wiped Out," while the story underneath noted that the extent of the loss of funds of the Anglican Church and St. John's College was "not known." By 29 August, the newspapers were reporting shortages of $1,250,000 in Church of England trust funds, and the *Free Press* ran a story headlined "College Council Fears Institution May Not Function." The careful reader of this latter story would discover that the St. John's College council was meeting on the matter that evening, and the doomsaying was from unnamed individual members rather than the council itself.

When the council did meet, it discovered that the situation was even worse than originally feared. A newspaper account of the meeting said the council had been informed that college funds were down $400,000, while the *Free Press* more alarmingly calculated the loss to the college at nearly $900,000. The warden presented a plan for carrying on, at least for the coming academic year. That plan involved mainly a small increase in tuition and massive cuts in salary for the entire staff, while leaving unsettled for the moment taxes, mortgage interest, and charges owed to the university, as well as small debts to tradesmen. A cable was sent to England to Canon Herklots—professor of church history and teacher of English—asking him whether he wished to return to Canada under the circumstances. The cable came back: "Returning. Herklots." Warden Wells was authorized to give a brief statement to the various newspapers that both the college and the school would carry on despite the disappearance of the college's investments, chiefly in Dominion of Canada National Service bonds.

In a letter of 9 May 1933, Warden Wells listed the schedule of salaries for 1932–33 and compared it with the rates paid before the defalcation:

	OLD RATE	NEW RATE
The Warden	$3600 with house	$1200 with house & fuel
Dean Matheson	$3600 with house	$1200 with house & fuel
Canon Gill	$2400 with house	$1200 with house & fuel
Canon Murray	$2400 with house	$1200 with house & fuel
Canon Herklots	$2400 with house	$1200 with house & fuel
Professor Cross	$2100 with Board	$600 with Board
Professor Baker	$1800 with Board	$600 with Board
Mr. T.C. Boon	$2100	$1200 with house & fuel
Rev. L.A.C. Smith	$900	$600
Miss Preudhomme	$600	

In his memoir Wells emphasized that all the teaching staff accepted the salary cuts without complaint. All staff was also put on one month's notice. The warden, moreover, commented in his memoir that many tradesmen forgave small bills entirely and discounted larger ones as a contribution to the college in its time of need.

The provincial government eventually announced that it would restore the university endowments, the scholarship funds, and the Rockefeller grant, but not the losses to the Dominion Land Grant. The Anglican Church and the college did not press charges against Machray despite losses of nearly $1 million. They did not "choose to add to Mr. Machray's ruin and [their] own embarrassment by instituting further prosecution," Archbishop Stringer was reported as saying. The government provided no assistance for St. John's College, but the national Anglican Church established the Restoration Fund of the Church of England in Canada, which over the next few years provided considerable amounts of money for the diocese through a national fundraising campaign. John Machray was sentenced to seven years in Stony Mountain and died there of cancer after a short incarceration. He insisted that he had not benefited personally from the stolen funds. Warden Wells and other Anglicans chose to believe that Machray had suffered from a long series of bad investments, and out of the goodness of his heart had continued to pay interest to his clients, robbing Peter to pay Paul in order to do so. That story still retains considerable currency among the older generation of Anglicans in the city. They obviously have not read carefully the report of the Royal Commission that investigated the defalcation.

Attempting to estimate the extent of the losses to the college, the real money value of those losses in 1932 dollars, and the effect over time of those losses to the endowment is an impossible task. Separating from the total the losses to the diocese and to the college was always itself well nigh impossible, partly because of the intertwining of the funds of the college and the cathedral. A best estimate is that the college probably lost something in the neighbourhood of $400,000. The professoriate's salaries after 1932 were around one-fiftieth of present-day salaries. If we multiply $400,000 by fifty, we get a figure of $20 million, which probably fairly approximates the modern buying power of what was lost in 1932. The college today would regard the raising of $20 million as virtually impossible. Even more complicated is the question of what the lost endowment would have become over the years if not embezzled. Carefully managed and invested, it might be worth in the hundreds of millions. There is no evidence that, however, even after Machray's sad example, the college was ever in a position to take advantage of careful financial management and investment. Existence was always too much on a hand-to-mouth basis, even in the good years.

From the beginning, the press assumed that Machray had experienced a series of bad investments, but had continued to pay interest to clients that was not actually received. A Royal Commission was appointed on 26 September 1932 to investigate the entire defalcation. It was composed of W.F.A. Turgeon of the Saskatchewan Court of Appeal, W.C. Murray, president of the University of Saskatchewan, and C.G.K. Nourse of Winnipeg, formerly of the Canadian Bank of Commerce. The inquiry lasted fifty-four days and heard from forty-four witnesses. It generally substantiated the earlier assumptions, but elaborated it by uncovering considerable evidence of Machray's deliberate machinations to keep afloat. The commission found total impairment to the university was $1,039,438, and another million was lost to other clients, mostly the Anglican Church and St. John's College. The commission claimed improper use of trust funds had begun as early as 1903 with the Isbister trust. Before 1924 sufficient securities could be allocated by Machray and Sharpe to the university accounts from its general pool of securities, and the commission only listed the losses to the university from 1925 to 1932 resulting from missing securities. The members of the university board of governors testified that they did not understand the intricacies of university finance and relied on Isaac Pitblado (to 1924) and then Machray to administer the system. So nobody was really in charge. So much for allowing businessmen to run the university! The final loss to the University Land Grant was calculated at $140,000. The depletion of the Isbister trust amounted to $80,397, and a number of other small funds were also depleted. The university in the 1920s had received a $12,000 Khaki University and YMCA endowment, and $507,000 from the Rockefeller Foundation for the medical faculty and another $80,000 for staff pensions. These three funds were almost entirely depleted.

A later study of the use made of the missing funds disclosed that about $300,000 of the two million had gone into Machray's personal accounts, but that he lived in a frugal manner. As had been suspected from the outset, most of the missing funds had covered investment losses. Funds were used to pay interest to clients on non-existent mortgages and investments to cover up the loss of the principal. Some funds were put into unsuccessful investment ventures, including a large farm near Meadows, Manitoba, managed by Machray. The commission found that every audited report from 1907 to 1917 was false, mostly because of the technique of delayed deposits (which amounted to $141,686 in 1913, the peak year). The delayed money, not deposited when received but held for many months, was used by the investment agents for their own purposes. The Machray firm deposited all its money received in a common trust account, which was used to finance investments and operating losses. Money was taken from this account every year to cover the delayed deposit position before the audit. After 1917 the auditors appeared to accept this method of operation as standard.

Beginning around 1911, Machray and Sharpe began using fictitious mortgages to account for trust investment. A client would receive a statement that his money was invested in such-and-such a mortgage and interest was paid to him on this mortgage. Any full audit of the trust accounts of Machray's firm at any time after 1911 would have disclosed insufficient assets to cover the liabilities. At the time of the closure of the firm's doors, it had assets of a mere $600 and liabilities of over $2 million. Machray and Sharpe was apparently bankrupt as early as 1912, at the end of the Winnipeg real estate boom of that year. Presumably Machray kept going by adopting illegal practices. There were no new misappropriations from 1917 to 1921 because of proper audits, but Machray got back into active embezzlement in 1921 and especially after 1924, when he became chairman of the board of governors. The commission put the principal blame on Machray and Sharpe themselves, but their employees were clearly complicit in the fraud. One employee in September 1932 claimed Machray had not speculated in the stock and grain markets, but had used poor judgement in land investments that suffered great depreciation. The Norris and Bracken governments, said the commission, ought not to have appointed Machray to plural offices.

The Turgeon investigation was much less concerned with the ways in which Machray had defrauded the Anglican Church and the college than it was with the explanation of the losses to the university. But it was clear that Machray had privately disposed of large amounts of securities supposedly held by the Anglican institutions, and had managed to cover up this disposition by preventing a proper audit of the securities, which would have involved their actual examination. As with the mortgages, he paid the interest up-to-date on the missing securities. He was able to stonewall on a proper audit because of the confidence virtually everyone shared in his probity and good will, and also because there was nobody prepared to ask the right questions, not even Warden Wells. Machray, after all, was the beloved college bursar for nearly ten years and a benefactor of the college of more than thirty years' standing.

A meeting of the college council on 15 September 1932 not only decided to continue the school, but also passed a motion that all cheques issued by the college and school had to be countersigned. It also agreed to accept the resignations of all the members of the council "in order to gain the full confidence and support of the church people of this diocese." Most were subsequently reappointed. For some unexplained reason, Warden Wells submitted to this meeting his utopian proposal for locating St. John's College at Fort Garry, probably to give those present at the meeting some hope for the future. The proposal was obviously unworkable at the moment.

Despite all the fiscal stringencies, college enrolment actually increased to 146 in 1932–33 and to 154 in 1933–34. The explanation for much of the increase was doubtless the move of third- and fourth-year students of the university to the Fort Garry campus at the same time as the news of

Machray hit the streets, leaving St. John's still in the North End and in close proximity to students living in that district. That college fees in these years were marginally lower than university ones also played its part. Most of the new enrolees were women, and two female faculty members were added to the staff, Miss Sybil Preudhomme (who taught modern languages) and Miss Marion Smith (Dean of Women and instructor in English). In 1935 the college added to its staff to teach history one of its most distinguished recent alumni and Rhodes Scholar, W.L. Morton. Thomas Boon added physics and chemistry to his registrar's duties, without receiving any additional salary.

As well as the short-term advantages to enrolment of the move of the university senior-level courses to the Fort Garry campus, a number of other factors mitigated the immediate impact of the Machray defalcation on the college. One was the Depression, which substantially reduced the financial expectations and cost of living of staff members. Warden Wells later reported that his family's live-in servant, having no other place to go, remained in his employment without pay. Another was the sympathy the entire community gave to the college in its hour of need. Finally, there was the Restoration Fund and the assistance of the Anglican Church. The Restoration Fund had raised $295,468.15 by early June 1933, most of it from outside the Winnipeg region, and organizers could talk of reaching $500,000 by the end of 1934. The organizers had done their best to insist that the college should do its own fundraising apart from the larger campaign. The council set the college's target at $125,000. The St. John's College Alma Mater Association held a special meeting to support the fund campaign, but soon discovered that many Old Boys of the school were not interested in the college. Council in April 1933 debated incorporating the school separately from the college, and the question of the future of the school was referred to committee, which reported that cooperation between school and college should continue as before. This would not last long. In any event, raising funds from Old Boys was not easy in the economic climate of 1933. Eric Hamber, for example, wrote from Vancouver, "I would never have thought it possible, with proper supervision, to have ever let him [John Machray] get away with what he did." The suggestion was that the college had a part in its own disaster. Certainly Hamber did not donate any money in 1933. Priority in the Restoration Fund was given to the restoration of the widows' and orphans' fund of the diocese, and St. John's College got some assistance from the proceeds. One major consequence of the fundraising kafuffle was the separation of the management of the school from that of the college in 1934. This separation produced a revised set of statutes in 1936. St. John's College School was poised to go its own way.

One of the many casualties of the new era of parsimony made necessary after 1932 was the library. An editorial in *The Johnian* in 1934 complained of the "absolute absence of a system of management, which would ensure the books being in the library for the students' use during the day." The problem, the editorial pointed out, was the lack of money to pay a librarian. The magazine advocated appointing students to act as librarians for the day, making sure that all books were properly checked out and locking the doors when no longer physically present.

Warden Wells reported to the archbishop on 15 May 1934 on his plan for the future. He recommended remaining in the present site for the next five to ten years. The government would not build for the college on the Fort Garry site, and any appeal to the public for funds would be, at the present, futile. In September 1934 the Episcopal and Clerical Sustenation Fund made a grant to the college of $2000 to help it carry on for the ensuing year. William Fraser, in his 1966 history of the college, wrote that the endowments had been fully replaced by the Restoration Fund, but this clearly was not quite the case. The college council wrote to the Carnegie Corporation in 1936 that "the lost endowments were restored but now yield approximately only half of the original revenue," and went on to emphasize that the teaching endowments—which amounted to more than $80,000 for four professorial chairs—had not been restored at all. This meant that teaching salaries had to be met chiefly out of current revenue. The loss of the teaching endowment is what distinguished the college from the schools. Both St. John's College School and Rupert's Land Ladies School had always funded teaching out of current registration revenue. The college had always enjoyed an endowment cushion. There is no record in the college papers of the numerical amount of the restored endowment fund, but in 1936–37 the warden told the council that endowments could provide a maximum of $5700 in revenue. Even at the reduced rates of interest of the Depression, this suggests an endowment fund of no more than $100,000.

Over the summer of 1934, Warden Wells received a telegram announcing that he had been unanimously elected Bishop of Cariboo. The decision to take the appointment was "an easy one," he wrote in his memoirs, and he resigned the wardenship effective 30 September 1934. Wells's departure was another blow to the college. The college would miss his energy. The archbishop announced that he would take over the wardenship, but because of his many duties would devolve the work on Prof. James Cross. Archbishop Stringer then died suddenly of a heart attack. During the critical 1934–35 period when fundraising most needed to be organized, therefore, the college was headed by an acting warden. Acting warden Cross proposed on 12 November that the college offer instruction in English, mathematics, Latin, French, German, history, and philosophy, as well as minors in religious education, economics, Greek, chemistry, and science, but refused to take the lead in soul-searching about the future. One of the few bright spots in this year was the decision by the board of Rupert's Land Ladies College to cover any deficits in the school's operating budget for the fiscal year. This was particularly useful since $21,834.25 of the school's capital fund had been involved in the defalcation. The college council itself recognized the necessity of appointing a warden. The Reverend Walter Barfoot, formerly professor and dean of residence at Emmanuel College, Saskatoon, had been appointed on 18 October 1934 as professor of church history at the college. Barfoot had graduated from Wycliffe College and had served as an officer in the Great War. His further appointment as warden was announced at a special meeting on 29 June 1935. Barfoot immediately presented to the council a review of the present situation and insisted "it would be necessary to review the general policy of the college at an early date."

By 1935 it was becoming increasingly clear that the college could no longer continue simply on the basis of belt-tightening. Blaming the defalcation for all the financial problems was tempting, but would have been far too simple. The fact was that even with the full income from the endowment, the college had been in precarious financial shape and falling farther behind every year. For some time annual operating expenses had been in the red, with shortfalls made up out of money transferred by Machray and Sharpe to the college. The ultimate question in the wake of the defalcation was always how the college would respond to its changed situation. In the short run, it could find ways to carry on. It had a teaching staff and some buildings. But carrying on would be hand-to-mouth and offered no place for growth and not much room for change. In some senses, the defalcation should have provided a wake-up call. Combined with the virtually simultaneous move of the senior part of the university to Fort Garry, it offered a golden opportunity to St. John's College to rethink its mandate and its vision. Warden Wells had recognized that "the future of the college" was a real and important question. But it needed to be met with a careful analysis of the present situation in the light of the college's past history, an honest appraisal of the college's assets and liabilities, and a concept of future direction that could be sold to a financially strapped public of alumni and well-wishers in the midst of a great depression.

Appraisal of the present situation should have led to a number of important conclusions. One was that both the city of Winnipeg and the province of Manitoba were—quite apart from the immediate economic problems of the Depression—at best stagnant and more than likely in the midst of a long-term period of decline. Winnipeg had lost its role as the warehouser to western Canada, while Manitoba agriculture was suffering from drought and badly weakened markets. Another conclusion should have been that Anglicanism in Winnipeg and Manitoba was also on the decline, partly for the same reasons that the city and province were, partly because traditional Christianity was in the midst of a long-term crisis of faith and commitment, and partly because the mother Anglican Church in Great

Britain had lost its way. Enthusiastic Anglican clergymen might convince themselves that the long-term trends could be turned around with enough belief and commitment, but they were simply whistling in the dark. No reason existed for assuming that an educational institution that specialized in training clergy for a church in western Canada in serious trouble was likely in the long run to flourish. The future had to be somewhere else, presumably in secular education.

Moreover, the history of the past quarter-century had certainly revealed that the Anglican diocese itself, Anglican parishioners of the diocese, alumni of the college, and the general Winnipeg public all lacked particularly strong affections or feelings for St. John's College, or at least did not have the sorts of affections that opened purse strings. Winnipeg businessmen had been sympathetic to the college's problems after the defalcation, but the Anglican community—facing its own financial crisis—was not. The bulk of the college's endowments that had been lost to John Machray's depredations had been raised mainly in England by his uncle, Archbishop Machray, before his death in 1904, when Manitoba and Winnipeg had been two of the fastest growing constituencies in the British Empire. The college had experienced great difficulty in the relatively prosperous times of the 1920s (which saw the beginning of the decline in Winnipeg and Manitoba) in raising endowments for the warden's salary or for the chair in religious education. *The Johnian* noted in 1934 that over the past few years the magazine had increasingly lost contact with the alumni. This loss of contact was not simply confined to the college magazine, however, but characterized the college as a whole. Outside organizations like the Carnegie and Rockefeller foundations had never been impressed by what the college had on offer—or at least with the amateurish ways what was on offer had been presented—and were unlikely to provide funding now, not least because of the disappearance into John Machray's bottomless pit of the large endowment the Rockefeller people had previously given to the university.

The college had some assets. It had a long and honoured history, and could legitimately claim to be the oldest institution of higher learning in western Canada. Its staff, alumni, and student body had been especially loyal to Canada and the British Empire during the Great War, and had paid heavily for that loyalty in loss of life. Whether this point could be translated into public support was another matter; its downsides were that a disproportionate number of Johnians were no longer around to prosper and donate money to financial appeals, and making a big deal out of heavy human contributions to the war effort would have been unseemly advertising. The college had a physical plant of some value, though the building was very expensive to heat, and a commitment from the province for space—presumably without charge—on the new Fort Garry campus. It also had a dedicated teaching staff, but one that contained no academic bright lights, although W.L. Morton might eventually become one. The situation was circular. "First-rate" faculty could not be attracted at present salaries and teaching conditions. Faculty that logged long hours in the classroom were what a college with a secure endowment could exploit. Faculty lacking outstanding reputations for academic excellence were not what a college fundraising desperately for its very existence needed. Even one faculty member with international standing, one single name the public had heard of, would have helped in a campaign. On the liability side, in addition to the mediocre earnestness of its teaching staff, the college had still not really worked out a suitable niche for itself within the University of Manitoba. It also had failed, as Warden Wells had admitted earlier to the Carnegie Foundation in 1925, in attracting its fair share of the province's Anglicans within its doors. Moreover, it was stuck resolutely in teaching the traditional liberal arts, another declining constituency.

In his subsequent report to the college board, Warden Barfoot tried to put the college's financial crisis "in proportion and perspective." The college faced an annual deficit and it was likely to increase. If more income was not generated or more money raised, he did not think the college could continue as a "full Arts and Theological College." He suggested the college "revert to the position of a Theological College and find less expensive premises." Barfoot thought the college was being too ambitious. Courses and staff needed to be cut. Because of the antiquated building the costs of heating were very high. He called for a council discussion of future policy. This should include, he insisted, a means of raising money to meet the "absolutely inescapable" deficit, and the future relationship of the college to the university.

The college decided once again to apply to the Carnegie people. This would provide a cheap fix that did not require much soul-searching, although its adoption demonstrated the unreal world in which the college lived in these years. The 1936 memorandum from the college council to the Carnegie Foundation, as well as emphasizing the college's financial shorts, also explained that the college had always expected to locate itself near the university site. It had purchased land downtown for this purpose, but the move of the university to Fort Garry had complicated matters. The move to Fort Garry and the restoration of teaching endowments would cost $500,000. Once on the campus, however, the memorandum went on, "we should be required to teach only Junior Division plus certain selected courses in the Senior Division and Theology." Only half the staff of the present location would be required. The college could teach senior division subjects not now given by the university—religious education, philosophy of religion, Hellenistic Greek, and Hebrew (enrolment grabbers, every one)—and the university could teach all the science. The college chapel would "bring the religious element into the full stream of University life." Carnegie rejected this application out of hand, although the head of the foundation visited Winnipeg early in 1937 and seemed well enough disposed toward the college.

The University of Manitoba celebrated its diamond jubilee in 1937. The event was decidedly a low-key one, at least as far as the college was concerned. One distinguished Johnian was selected to receive an honourary degree at the university's convocation, and a jubilee edition of academic essays was published. W.L. Morton, who was teaching history at St. John's, was chosen by the warden to contribute to the essays volume, and produced an essay on the history of Red River. In April 1937 the college learned to its dismay that the diocese had decided to undertake serious renovation of the fabric of the cathedral, so closely connected with the college through the canons. The canons agreed to become responsible for the restoration, which meant that they would get no income for years from any endowments and other funds set aside for them and the cathedral. Even more controversially, the diocese had determined that the college would share in the reallocation of deanship and chapter funds, on the grounds that "it would be easier to appeal for the College than it would be for the cathedral." As a result, the college, having dismally failed to raise money in North America, determined on a fundraising campaign in the old country as a possible solution to its new financial problems. Warden Barfoot himself would prepare the ground for the appeal by organizing the overseas graduates of the college on a visit to England in the capacity of financial agent. The warden himself insisted that most of the funds would have to be raised in Canada by a special appeal to the theological side of the work of the college. At a meeting of council on 8 July, the college agreed to waive its share of any life insurance money coming to John Machray's widow in order to avoid litigation with Mrs. Machray. The hope of the college for help from a new organization called "St. John's Messengers," a group of Anglican laymen whose work was intended to raise funds and increase enrolment, was not fully realized. The first council meeting of the academic year 1937–38 reported another enrolment shortfall.

In his interim report on his progress at the 13 September 1937 meeting, Warden Barfoot emphasized that English churchmen had lost almost all contact with western Canada since the turn of the century, when the last financial appeal had been made. Part of the problem was that missionary society connections had been entirely lost. The Church Missionary Society had withdrawn from Canada, and the Society for the Propagation of the Gospel had no commitments in Rupert's Land. The archbishop talked about the reopening of the missionary connections, and the Society for the Propagation of the Gospel had agreed to accept a deputation over the winter, but many in the Old Country were wary. The warden reported that the Society for the Promotion of Christian Knowledge had offered to allow him to preach an appeal. Nevertheless, the need for action on the English front was urgent, as another international missionary appeal would begin in 1940 and all fundraising for local colleges would have to cease. The international missionary effort, especially in Africa, was much more successful than the missionary campaign in North America. These realities of barren ground and lack of cultivation should have led the college's supporters to re-evaluate and reject the idea of raising funds in England. They did not.

Much debate in council did occur over the business of sending the warden to England. Some thought it an unnecessary financial burden, while others argued that "the Council was at the crossing of the roads and that it was a case of now or never." Everyone agreed that in order to keep the arts and theological sides of the college in operation, another fundraising campaign was necessary. Mr. J.W.E. Armstrong, one of the leading laymen on the council, insisted the campaign be undertaken on both sides of the Atlantic. Warden Barfoot favoured the English appeal, on the grounds that the Restoration Fund and the drought had exhausted western Canada of money to donate. The archbishop counselled optimism on the financial side because something had to be done. He said he would hold a dinner and "put the case for the College before a number of those likely to be interested." The dinner was duly held at the Manitoba Club, and the archbishop was encouraged by the response of those attending, although he did not offer any numbers as to the amount of money actually pledged. Despite the personal efforts of Archbishop Harding and an expensive advertising campaign in 1938, Barfoot's efforts barely paid their expenses. The best that Barfoot could report to the council was that "the people in England were now aware that St. John's College is a missionary institution and part of their missionary obligation." The years of 1938 and 1939, of course, were not prime years for raising money for educational institutions in remote parts of North America.

Meanwhile, the college enrolment began again to be a problem. It had dropped to eighty-one in 1938–39. The college council in 1938 had rejected the idea of the graduate society that the college recruit more actively in the high schools among non-Anglican and new Canadian students, on the grounds that such a campaign might "antagonize the Educational Department." The council did agree to an increase in publicity for St. John's through the diocesan women's associations. Financial difficulties continued to dominate the meetings of council. Bursar Boon reported in May 1939 an accumulated deficit of $11,192, which would soon have to be liquidated and creditors paid. Boon insisted that "some decision on the question of whether or not we are to open next fall must be made without delay." He maintained that in order to continue, the college should not only pay its creditors but be assured somehow that similar deficits would not arise again. The short-run crisis could be met by sale of assets, both buildings and bonds. The possibility of assurance for the future came, he thought, mainly from staff retirements. The question of continuation was rendered more urgent by an offer of $40,000 for the college building, with possession by 30 May 1940. Obviously the sale of the building would at the very least require a move to another site.

Over the summer of 1939, the college council also heard from a committee appointed earlier to discuss amalgamation with Ravenscourt School that overtures from Ravenscourt had recently been made. The council's conditions for such an amalgamation included stipulations that the new institution be known as "St. John's College School" and that it remain an Anglican institution. It would be later reported that Ravenscourt was not interested in such terms. The archbishop thought $75,000 would be required to complete the merger of the two schools. Sale of building and the merger were obviously connected, and the debate in council on these questions was a lively one. The warden pointed out that 98 percent of the day students at the college came from the North End of Winnipeg. Moving the college from its present location would mean "an entirely fresh start in every sense of the term," he predicted. In the end, the motion to sell the college building failed on 22 June 1939.

Also in 1939 the college voted to change the hood for the bachelor of divinity degree. The motion was that the hood "be of Cambridge (or full) shape, and of black silk, the tippet to have square corners. That the lining should be gold silk throughout, and that there be a green silk cord of piping from the edge all round and carried over the neck band, including the tippet." The incongruity of this cosmetic change in the midst of disaster did not appear to strike the council.

World War II, which began in September 1939, was not kind to St. John's College. From the outset, the college knew that war would reduce enrolment and increase costs. The council was told there was no chance of windfall money from England—which was virtually bankrupt—and the only option for the college school was to canvass Old Boys for a $50,000 endowment fund. That campaign seemed to arouse some interest. It was to culminate in October 1940, at the 120th anniversary of the founding of the school. Appeals for the college proper through the city's churches were less promising, however, and the difference between the enthusiasm of the Old Boys and the lack of commitment of the alumni and church people was palpable. The chairman of this campaign reported that appeals for the college "were left to one side owing to the multiplicity of appeals for War Organizations and other purposes which seem to be being made continually." The appeal would have to be broadened, he suggested, although no suggestions were made as to how this could be effected. In the short run, enrolment rose in 1939–40, with sixty-five new students (forty-two men and twenty-three women). The rise was chiefly owing to the introduction of the teaching of second-year chemistry and physics. There might have been a lesson in this increase, but nobody ever proposed one. The warden himself admitted in a report to council in October 1939 that "the attitude of the average churchman towards appeals for St. John's College appears to be that the responsibility for Arts education rests with the State, and that he ought not to be asked to support an Institution in competition with those he is already supporting." Interestingly enough, added the warden, the authorities at the University of Manitoba seemed to be more favourably disposed to the college than lay Anglicans. The warden also insisted that there was no evidence that the Anglican community would respond more sympathetically to an appeal for a theological college. The solution, concluded Warden Barfoot, was an adequate per capita grant from public funds, but the government was unwilling to do this for obvious political reasons. Using public funds to support directly denominational higher education would have touched off much criticism in the province.

One committee after another investigated the state of the college and offered its well-meaning recommendations. The result of council discussion on the future of the college in October 1939 (immediately after the outbreak of war) was the appointment of a "Special Commission to Investigate the Affairs of St. John's College and the Operation Thereof," which reported back to council in June 1940. This commission began by raising the question of whether the continuation of St. John's College at its present geographical location was justified, given the number of similar institutions in existence. It observed that the college had hoped to get money from England, which, in view of the present war, seemed most unlikely. The commission felt that continual deficits could not be allowed to continue, however. It proposed, not a final solution, but an interim one, based on the assumption that the war would not cause a "disastrous decline in enrolment." It maintained that the management systems at the college schools had improved the financial situation by reducing expenses, and it recommended a similar creation of a board of management for the college (along with the elimination of the present services of the registrar and steward).

A management committee for the college was duly created and met frequently over the summer of 1940. It began with the intention of maintaining the full arts course at the college, but it soon discovered that with the public schools now offering free grade 12, it would be virtually impossible to continue the full arts offerings. Instead, the committee ended up not only recommending that the college operate only as a theological department with limited provision of arts subjects for the theological students, but actually moving forward on this plan. The committee emphasized that this decision was only for the duration of the war. Council accepted the committee's action, although it complained that such an important question should have been placed before it.

In February 1941 the college received the final dispersal from the bankruptcy administration of Machray and Sharpe. It amounted to $3500. The same council meeting also received the resignation of Warden Barfoot, who had been elected bishop of Edmonton. He was replaced by Canon R.S.K. Seeley, who had been teaching in the college. Over the summer of 1941, a special committee on St. John's College was appointed by the synod of the diocese and met "to understand the problem presented to us and our duty concerning it." The report of this committee made manifest trends in diocesan-college relations that had previously remained unspoken. Clearly the college had failed to maintain connections with the diocese, as it had also failed with its graduates. This committee made a number of important recommendations. Firstly, the committee argued that the college should look entirely to the university for the arts course. "It does not seem to the Committee necessary, desirable, or possible to re-establish this department of the Institution." Times had changed since the college had been founded. The committee noted that other church institutions in eastern Canada had been dealt with in a similar fashion. The committee further recommended that the college should concentrate entirely on the teaching of theology, on educating young men for the ministry. Thirdly, the committee wanted St. John's College "moved into a more central position in the life of the Provincial University." How a theological school could become an important force on a secular campus was not explained. Fourthly, the committee argued that the college must move closer to the membership of the diocese. "There is a certain remoteness of the College from the Church people," opined the committee, and it had to be bridged. The report blamed the remoteness partly on the overwork of the faculty, but also on the fact that most clergy in the diocese had been educated elsewhere. Finally, it called for a new body to be called something like "Friends of the College," delegates of which would be elected by the parishes. Clearly the college could expect no financial assistance, and probably precious little moral support, from the diocese of Rupert's Land. One might have expected the leadership of the college to draw some conclusions from this series of committee reports. But hope springs eternal.

As if directly challenging the diocesan report, Warden Seeley announced in a press release the program of the college for the 1941–42 academic year. All arts subjects offered during the past year would be offered again, and he hoped for additional English and history courses that would permit students to take a full arts course in the senior division at the college. He denied that St. John's was ceasing to be an arts college at the university, and added that given sufficient support, the college would soon offer again a full arts course in both the junior and senior divisions. Instead, St. John's joined with the other affiliated colleges in requesting a share of the examination fees charged by the University of Manitoba, pointing out that the colleges supplied more than 50 percent of the examining committees in arts and sciences. Yet another committee was appointed in March 1942 to consult on the present position of the college under wartime conditions and to discuss the possibilities for the future. Two months later, the warden reported on the future policy of the college. He noted that the college had maintained its status as an arts college of the university with some senior division work. But virtually the entire senior division was graduating. To build up a new student body, he argued that the junior division must now be emphasized. Therefore, he argued for a full junior division and a grade 12 course. This program would work only with sixty-five students or fundraising of $3000. An animated discussion on this report emphasized that the diocese as a whole needed to recognize its responsibility toward the college, and the warden subsequently presented the same report to the diocesan synod.

In the spring of 1943 Warden Seeley resigned and was replaced by R.J. Pierce, formerly rector of St. Barnabas Church, Calgary. Pierce took up his duties in August 1943. The academic year 1943–44 saw a further drop in enrolment to twenty-nine students, and council decided to move to a site nearer the university at the earliest opportunity. In January 1944 the college chancellor and warden met with President Sidney Smith of the University of Manitoba at the Manitoba Club to discuss the future. Smith urged St. John's not to make a permanent move at this time, since he expected that the junior division on Broadway would close and the federal government would make grants available for a new building. He advised the college to lobby with the province for a share of the reconstruction money he expected to become available. He suggested the rental of a suitable new home near the city centre, and the continuation of arts teaching because of "the necessity for the maintenance of integrity in the field of liberal education, no matter what future political changes might occur in the country." Smith had always been one of the prominent educators in Canada who actively supported the liberal arts. Not long after this meeting, college council authorized the sale of the college building in the North End.

By the 1944–45 academic year, enrolment had plunged to twenty-five, mostly females, and the college had put most of its extracurricular activities and social life on hold for the duration. The extent of the courses offered continued to be a tribute to the hard work of a small cadre of dedicated faculty. As had been true during World War I, the college honour roll was certainly a long one, with 158 names by 1945, including thirteen students and one lecturer who had been killed in the conflict. As for moving, council at first entertained an offer from the Peretz School and the Jewish Folk School for the building. Negotiations were not successful, and in December 1944 the council voted to accept an offer from the Ukrainian Greek Orthodox Church of Canada. The problem then became the finding of a new location, under circumstances of urgency and general shortage of space in Winnipeg. President Smith of the university recommended that the college remain downtown until the university had actually moved its junior division, which would occur soon after the war. In early February 1945, United College offered to provide St. John's with temporary accommodation, but the college rejected it because of the "enormous danger of St. John's College being completely swallowed up by United College." Instead, after a careful survey of available real estate, the college fixed on the university's Music and Arts Building on the corner of Broadway Avenue and Hargrave Street, formerly the home of J.H. Ashdown. This site had the great merit of being adjacent to the university's junior division. It was also closer to the college's Anglican constituency, which now resided in River Heights, Fort Rouge, St. Vital, and Crescentwood, and more often attended United College than St. John's College. The college purchased this building for $70,000 and proposed to move into it for the 1945–46 academic year. With the war ending and with a better location than before, the college could hope to march successfully into the post-war period.

Chapter Eight

On Broadway, 1945–1958

As World War II concluded, St. John's College staggered to a new down-town location, its future most insecure. The hope was that the institution would be able to participate in the enrolment boom that would accompany reconstruction after the war. It moved to its new quarters at the corner of Broadway Avenue and Hargrave Street during the first week in July 1945, in between ve Day and vj Day. The completion of renovations was rendered extremely difficult by the great shortage of labour in Winnipeg at this time; the war was winding down and reconstruction had already begun, putting enormous pressure on the building industry. The renovations were made by the Bird Construction Company, and most of the total cost ($16,500) was forgiven by Anglican layman H.J. Bird, leaving a bill for only $5000. The building was ready for lectures on time, and the residence was sold out. Both the boys' school and the girls' school reported record enrolment for the 1945–46 academic year, including large numbers of boarders. The school was obviously heading in its own direction apart from the college. Walter Burman was appointed organizing secretary of the Campaign for Building the New School, probably on a site in Tuxedo already purchased. Surely the corner had been turned!

By the spring of 1946, it was clear that staffing considerations would be an important matter. The college had operated with an aging teaching contingent, supplemented by part-time hirings, for many years. These people had taught long hours and been greatly underpaid. Many had already stepped down or were ready to step down. New hiring would have to face up to heavy competition from the United States. American universities were snapping up junior men at unheard-of salaries (over $4000 per year!), and Canada would have to keep pace. A new salary and teaching hours schedule was drawn up in May 1946:

Department	Salary	Teaching Hours
Warden	$2400 & rooms	18 plus administration
English	$3000	14
Modern Languages	$2100	24
History and Economics	$1500	16
Mathematics and Science	$2000	19
Philosophy	$2400	16
Psychology & Sociology	$2400	14
Latin (& assist English)	$2400	17
Greek	$900 Board & room	18
Church History	$300	2
Reserve for extra assts.	$500	

Most of the major personnel components of this module had yet to be hired, but it gives a fair idea of the sort of curriculum being proposed for the post-war period: a standard liberal arts offering. The teaching loads, while heavy by modern standards, were typical of liberal arts colleges of the time in both Canada and the United States. The subsequent appointments made included W.P. Wilgar (MA, Cantab, formerly of Mount Allison); O.S. White (BA, Amherst, from Puerto Rico); Dr. Cook (D.Ed., Harvard, from Sir George Williams); Douglas Silverston (BA, B.Litt, Oxon.); and Mr. James Jackson (BA Hons., Manitoba, from the Manitoba Provincial Archives). Most of these appointments were gone within a year or two, however. The new appointments were put on the University of Manitoba graded rank system, and a pension plan was subsequently offered to the lay members of staff, based on the college's matching a 5 percent contribution to a pension fund. That both a ranking system and a pension plan had to be freshly introduced in 1946 suggests the previous reliance of the college on the canons and churchmen. Registration for the 1946–47 academic year was 117 students, forty in theology and pre-theology. As evidence of the new vigour being exhibited everywhere, a play presented by the college won a series of awards at the Winnipeg Dramatic Festival. And as evidence of a new spirit of optimism as far as long-term enrolment was concerned, the college council voted to cease the provision of grade 12 by the college. Such euphoria was to be short-lived, however.

By the beginning of the 1947–48 academic term, the bloom was already off the post-war renaissance of St. John's College. Enrolment had dropped to under thirty. For an institution still heavily dependent upon registrations to pay teaching salaries, the drop was a disaster and almost totally unexpected. In the centennial history William Fraser argues that the college had failed to recruit very well among the children of Anglicans, apparently on the assumption that Anglicans had been a specially targeted group for recruitment. Perhaps it would be more accurate to say that St. John's failed to mount any sort of successful campaign for students among any potential clientele, Anglicans included. In fairness, nobody on the staff knew anything about recruiting students. The process in 1947 had followed the usual non-proactive pattern. The doors were swung open. The college sent out discreet (and inexpensive) announcements to the local media, mainly the diocesan ones. In any event, the debate over the report of the finance committee on 16 December 1947 at a very well-attended meeting of council (twenty-seven members were present, including delegates from the diocese) resulted in an all-too-familiar motion, "That a campaign be undertaken to raise funds to meet the deficit anticipated in the budget." The present deficit was more than $12,700 on an anticipated revenue of $33,504.

The synod delegates subsequently introduced a series of recommendations that represented the local layman's view of how to fix the college. These included a recommendation that St. John's become a theological college only, with an added hostel for arts students, as well as another motion asking for a move of the college to the Fort Garry campus. The proposition that St. John's College teach only theology was in some ways an attractive one. Warden Pierce had revised and modernized the theological course over the years. In 1945 he had extended the training time of the Licentiate of Theology from two to three years and raised the number of theology courses in the process. By 1948 the college had a pre-theology program, as well as a theology one educating a number of former servicemen. Synod also wanted more attention paid to the rural ministry and more emphasis on rural work and agriculture by the theological school. Another all-too-familiar motion also made its inevitable appearance at this council meeting, that "a subcommittee be appointed to consider the future policy of the College."

And so yet another committee report was submitted on 26 January 1948 on the "possible courses of future action" to overcome the difficulties facing St. John's College. This subcommittee heard a number of briefs and statements. One from the warden called for the continuation of arts courses if at all possible, in obvious contradiction to the synod's recommendations. The warden also introduced an estimated budget for the operation of a college junior division plus theological school. This option produced an estimated deficit of $3625. Another from a special subcommittee produced an estimated budget for the diocesan solution: the operation of a theological college and a residence for university students. This option would run at a deficit of $2441. All options would produce a deficit; the difference was in the amount that would have to be independently raised. A report from financial advisor Mr. A.E. Hoskins stated that the trust monies of the college would still be available so long as St. John's College existed under its present name and as "an independent educational institution functioning within the Province of Manitoba." The trusts were no impediment to dropping secular education. An offer was also tabled from United College, suggesting that if St. John's sent its senior students to them, they would allow "generous concessions" on the fees. The subcommittee did not offer a final solution. Instead it recommended that the college choose either to teach only junior division arts and theology, or to teach theology alone. In either case, the residence would continue to be operated, and any vacancies would be offered to other university students. The subcommittee also insisted that whatever option was chosen, the college would have to be energetically promoted as to registration, there would have to be a vigorous appeal to the alumni, church people would have to be solicited, and operating expenses would have to be cut to the bone, even if this meant cooperating with United College by sharing staff. The subcommittee offered no recommendations about a move to Fort Garry, partly because there was no available information from the university on what aid it might provide for such a step.

The council moved into committee of the whole to consider this report, breaking for supper and reconvening at 7:00 p.m. The result was a successful motion scrapping senior-level teaching "during the next session." The further decision about whether to continue with junior arts was deferred until a meeting could be held with the University of Manitoba on the terms by which the college would be greeted at the Fort Garry site. (Informal enquiries would lead to meetings with the university's finance committee. Out of these would come a resolution of the university's board of governors on 12 February 1948 that the university "offer St. John's College a free site at Fort Garry, with the privilege of using all services such as heat, electric light and water at cost, and using dining rooms, laundry and other services on the same basis as those services are used by the departments of the University.") In the meantime it was announced that a generous friend of the college had offered $5000 to help cover the present deficit, providing a fundraising campaign matched it. Over the next few months, the college moved belatedly in some obvious directions. A meeting in March 1948 saw the establishment of a committee on promotion and publicity, to be chaired by the warden. An alumni committee was formed over the summer of 1948, chaired by Prof. W.L. Morton, who was now a member of the history department at the university, which compiled a mailing list of the names of 450 alumni. That the college had been fundraising for years without such committees—or an alumni mailing list—speaks volumes for its relationship with its graduates. Less creatively, the college administration once again tried the Carnegie Foundation and the Rockefeller Foundation for funds, this time to finance the move to Fort Garry. The answer from both foundations was a polite "no."

For the 1948–49 academic year, arts instruction was given only in the junior division. Enrolment in arts stood at eighteen, and in theology at twenty-two. In the residence there were twenty-five men. On 8 June 1949, the long search of the college school for a new site was finally answered by a successful motion to college council that "steps be taken to effect the amalgamation of St. John's College Boys' School and Ravenscourt Boys' School." The school building and property had been sold and would have to be turned over to the buyer in 1950. The proceeds had not generated enough money to build on the Tuxedo site acquired earlier by the school. Instead, the two schools would be combined to form a new school, St. John's-Ravenscourt, on the present Ravenscourt site in Fort Garry. One of the implications of this merger was that the long-standing relationship between St. John's College and St. John's College School would be finally severed. The negotiations between the two schools dragged on for some months before becoming finalized.

At the start of the 1949 academic year, the college council was unexpectedly visited by an all-star delegation of officials from the University of Manitoba, including chancellor A.K. Dysart, board of governors president W.J. Parker, and university president A.H.S. Gilson. By this time the university had decided to move its junior division from the downtown campus to Fort Garry over the summer of 1950. The university administration had also decided to take the lead with all the colleges, inviting them to make their homes at Fort Garry. President Gilson offered the St. John's Council "a series of thoughts concerning the future development of University education in the Province of Manitoba," a vision of a St. John's College sited at Fort Garry, and invited the college to move. Dysart and Parker also addressed the council. In the formal language of the council minutes, a motion was made thanking the visitors and accepting "the principles involved in the scheme outlined." At a council meeting on 12 October, it was announced that enrolment was eleven in first-year arts, nine in second-year arts, and twenty in theology. The warden also reported that the deficit had finally been eliminated. Against this background, the warden made the motion that the archbishop appoint a committee to "continue negotiations with the University of Manitoba on the basis of the President's statement to the Council." It passed easily.

So yet another committee would examine the future of St. John's College. This one, headed by Warden Pierce, reported that the University of Manitoba was irrevocably committed to Fort Garry. While some branches were still elsewhere, the big concentration of students would be on that site. The committee further pointed out that theological education in the modern world was increasingly becoming associated with universities. At Fort Garry, the college's arts students could have access to a larger library, a much larger company of fellow students, and much greater extracurricular activities. For the college, the report added, the clinching argument in favour of the Fort Garry site was the influence it could have on the student body of the university, with a chapel on campus and regular service for students, as well as courses in religious knowledge. The college had been sympathetic to moving to the site of the university for many years, but had not done so. In 1945 when the college had moved its building, the university had advised it to wait a few years to settle its plans. The move to Broadway had worked out quite well, argued the committee. "It was the rising cost of salaries and all the things we had to buy, decreasing returns from investments, and no increase in Arts fees which compelled us to limit our courses drastically and thereby reduce our enrolment by more than fifty per cent just at a time when we appeared to be on the verge of a larger enrolment than ever." Now the university was ready for St. John's College. The committee emphasized that it was nice to feel wanted. The university would offer complete services and even the use of university classrooms. The university hoped to establish a university college so that registration would become possible by colleges rather than by faculties. The college would have to erect a chapel, a residence, and provision for faculty accommodation, a few classrooms, and the theological library. The committee concluded that the move was possible, and observed that the university had offered to purchase the Broadway building at a fair price. One of the reasons the university was so welcoming in the spring of 1950, of course, was because it had finally committed itself to moving the junior division from the Broadway campus to the Fort Garry campus over the summer of that year. St. John's College and the Roman Catholic St. Paul's College, established in 1926, would be left downtown, while access to advanced-level courses by their students would become much more difficult.

Warden Pierce was the individual who had to sell to the diocese this vision of a great college at Fort Garry, for in truth he was the person who had responded with most enthusiasm to the university's invitation. He made his attempt at the diocesan synod in May 1950. After much debate, the motion to support the college's plan to move to the campus was rejected. In his enthusiasm, Pierce had forgotten the extent of the opposition in the diocese to the college and especially to its continuation as a liberal arts college. He probably should have spent a year lobbying for the plan instead of going so quickly to the synod with it. Depressed by his defeat, Pierce readily accepted an offer to become bishop of Athabasca, and he was consecrated in September 1950, leaving the college once again leaderless, this time at the opening of the 1950–51 academic year.

At this point the college might well have died. But Archbishop Sherman had one final possibility. He contacted Laurence Wilmot, who had just settled into a parish in Winnipeg after four years' service with the Anglican

Board of Religious Education. The negotiations had to be carried out in secret, for Sherman did not want to tip his hand prematurely. Wilmot was a graduate of St. John's who had served with distinction as a military chaplain in Italy. He had been decorated for bravery under fire. He was personable, persuasive, and incredibly energetic, sustained in all his efforts by his deep faith in God. He believed in the importance of a liberal education and was reluctant to take on the job, less because of the monumental challenge it presented than because he felt inadequately prepared and educated to head an academic institution. He accepted Archbishop Sherman's invitation, however, and joined the college as warden in November 1950.

Wilmot's selection was placed before the college council as a *fait accompli* because the archbishop feared the council would not support carrying on. His task was to be patient, keeping the college afloat while building up support among the clergy and laity of the diocese prior to another proposal to the synod to move to the Fort Garry site. Like every other person involved in higher education in Canada—but not many Anglicans of the diocese— Wilmot knew full well that the demography of the country was running in his favour. Within a few years of his taking office, there would begin to be enormous pressure from young people upon all Canadian colleges and universities as a baby boom, which had begun in 1939, reached the level of higher education. Not only would there be a larger pool of university-age Canadians, but, because of the earlier introduction of more or less universal secondary school education in Manitoba, more of them would want to go on to higher education. We know a good deal about the behind-the-scenes life of the college during the 1950s because of a frank memoir written by Wilmot (and recently published by St. John's College Press).

The new warden and his family moved into an apartment in the college building on Broadway, which was definitely showing its age. In the first year, he and his eldest son had to shovel coal into the ancient furnace on weekends to keep the place warm. A small fire in the walls during the winter nearly led to utter disaster. Beyond this, the real problems started. The teaching staff consisted of six full-time faculty members. One of these was supposed to teach several theological courses but was better equipped to teach English literature; the warden himself taught the theology, putting thirteen hours a week in the classroom. In addition there was one part-time instructor, Ted Scott, the future Primate of All Canada, who taught psychology and Old Testament. Enrolment consisted of twenty men in training for the ministry, ten in their last year, and only seven arts students. The income from registration was so small that Wilmot would again have to go out into the business community hat in hand, as former warden Pierce had done since 1945, to collect funds to meet the bills. Most of the Anglican community really thought that the college should close its doors, and sat on its wallets.

In the spring of 1951, the college caught an enormous break, which would ease the new warden's task considerably. On 19 June 1951, responding to the coming shortfall in university places, the Canadian Parliament decided to appropriate $7 million for higher education in Canada. For the first time, the Dominion would become involved in university funding. Grants could not be more than fifty cents per head of student population, and the grant was to be divided in each province among eligible institutions according to the ratio of their enrolment of eligible students to the total number of students enrolled. The appropriations were a direct result of recommendations by the Commission on Arts, Letters, and Science chaired by Vincent Massey, which had examined culture in Canada during 1949 and 1950. (Massey as Governor General would lay the cornerstone for the new University of Manitoba library on 28 October 1952; it would open on 26 September 1953.) Under this scheme, the province of Manitoba in 1951 got $388,250, based on a population of 776,500. The University of Manitoba, with its 2828 students, got $279,151.75, and its affiliated colleges, with 1104 students, got $109,098.25. The grants, nearly $100 per student, were paid directly to the various educational institutions involved, including the University of Manitoba's affiliated colleges. St. John's College initially received only a few thousand dollars a year, but the grant was sufficiently large—and dependable—to enable the college later in the decade to operate without the constant desperation of the 1940s. While these grants were important sources of funding for every institution of higher education in the land, in Manitoba they were particularly welcomed by the denominational colleges, all of which had been experiencing considerable financial difficulties. The grants made possible a renewed energy in the colleges throughout the decade of the 1950s.

Warden Wilmot worked very hard at increasing enrolment, particularly since the government grant was tied to it. From the beginning of his wardenship he actively recruited students in Anglican parishes right across the diocese, within Winnipeg and without, selling his vision of St. John's as an Anglican liberal arts and theological college. In 1951 he was forced to face dissent behind his back. One of his senior faculty members convinced influential clergymen in the diocese (and the archbishop) that the warden had stirred up considerable discontent within the college and could no longer manage it. The situation became so tense that Wilmot actually resigned at one point, but the archbishop discovered that the only discontent was confined to one senior faculty member, who probably had expected to become the new warden himself, and too much credence had been given to his complaints. Wilmot retracted his resignation and stayed on at his job.

Enrolment grew slowly but steadily. In 1951, in addition to twenty theological students, there were thirteen in junior arts and science. Wilmot realized that senior arts and science would have to be increased, and by 1952 he had forty students, twelve in first-year arts, nine in second-year arts, nine in senior arts, and ten theologues. Increased numbers meant further pressure on space, as well as more money from the government grant, and the Wilmot family moved out of the Broadway building in 1953, a year distinguished by several other important developments. One was a total overhaul of the college statutes by council, the first major revision since the institution had been founded by Bishop Machray in 1866. Another important move was the appointment of a committee (consisting of the chancellor, the warden, and Prof. W.L. Morton) to consult with the university administration and determine future policy regarding a move to the campus. The university administration continued to be most enthusiastic about the future of St. John's College, which was a pleasant contrast with the attitude of Manitoba's Anglican community. On 2 November 1953, Walter Foster Barfoot was installed as the college's chancellor as part of his duties as newly appointed archbishop of Rupert's Land. As a former warden of the college, Barfoot could be expected to be sympathetic to its problems and supportive of a future relocation to the Fort Garry campus.

By 1954, the Broadway building was full to overflowing. The college needed a women's residence and more classrooms. It moved to purchase an old, white, brick and stone building next door to the existing building, on the corner of Carlton and Broadway, acquired in 1945. Warden Wilmot found raising a $30,000 mortgage to be very difficult. He was finally informed by his businessmen contacts that the problem was that the Anglican community was confused by this expansion. Everyone expected the college to move to Fort Garry, and what was it doing buying more property downtown? Wilmot replied that the space really was needed in the short run, adding that the new building would complete a block on Broadway and make the property much more attractive when it was eventually put on the market. Everyone understood this logic, and the new acquisition was quickly funded. The college thus opened the 1954–55 academic year with its first women's residence in place, and an enrolment of fifty-eight students, including a young man from eastern Manitoba named Ed Schreyer, eventually to become provincial premier and Governor General, as well as several future bishops. The enrolment included eighteen men and ten women in first year.

The autumn of 1954 was distinguished in several senses. One important occasion was an unexpected visit from Dr. Geoffrey Fisher, the Archbishop of Canterbury, who was touring western Canada. Fisher very graciously introduced himself as an alumnus of the college, since he had received an honourary degree a few years earlier. Another equally key event was a visit by Warden Wilmot and W.L. Morton to the incoming president of the University of Manitoba, Hugh H. Saunderson, who proved as keen as his predecessor to welcome St. John's to the Fort Garry campus. The Wilmot regime had sufficiently raised the profile and the respectability of the college that diocesan leaders, including Archbishop Barfoot, were willing to reconsider the earlier negative vote at the synod. At a very full council meeting on 9 December 1954, plans for a serious college fundraising campaign were recommended by the committee of promotion and public relations. These included the designation of a Sunday in January to be observed throughout the diocese as St. John's College Sunday; the formation of a virtual "convocation" to include all students, graduates, and alumni, as well as friends of the college; and the organization of a major fundraising event at the college in the spring. Mrs. George (Peggy) Sellers and Mrs. W.A. Folliott, both good friends of the college, were put in charge of mounting such an event. A letter from the board of governors of the university was read, reaffirming the earlier offer of land suitable for a site for St. John's College on the campus. Archbishop Barfoot as chancellor then told the meeting that the time to decide the question of moving had come. Ted Scott moved the motion "that this College Council affirms that its future policy is to move to the Fort Garry Campus as soon as satisfactory arrangements can be made and that the Chancellor be hereby authorized to set up a committee to consider this matter." This motion passed unanimously.

From this point on, events moved very swiftly towards the relocation of the college. Word of the action of council spread rapidly through the Winnipeg business community, and Warden Wilmot soon had on his desk an offer for the Broadway property of $85,000. He managed to raise the offer, which was from Monarch Life Assurance Company, to $175,000 cash, and college council, at a meeting on 25 January 1955 considered this offer carefully. Wilmot argued that the property was worth more and that the college should hold out for at least $200,000, but most of the council were leery of such "greedy" tactics and opted to accept the existing offer. (Wilmot later learned that the bidders had expected to go to $200,000.) In the final arrangements, carried out by the chancellor, the college would have at least three years to prepare its move to Fort Garry before vacating the premises.

Only a few days later, on 7 February, a major meeting was held between the university authorities and the college leadership, which worked out most of the details of the college's occupancy at Fort Garry. The arrangement was very favourable to the college, especially on the issue of academic autonomy, demonstrating how serious the university was about attracting St. John's (and, it hoped, other colleges) to the rural campus. At the same time, the deal was so good for the college that there was soon backlash within faculties and departments critical of the concessions that the university had made, and the college would eventually pay for the generosity of the original offer when the terms were renegotiated in the later 1960s. On this subsequent occasion, the university was not disposed to be at all sympathetic to college autonomy.

In any event, in 1955 the college was offered a choice of three parcels of land on a ninety-nine-year renewable lease on the Fort Garry campus, and chose the present site on Dysart Road. The archbishop indicated that the college was thinking about constructing a residence for up to 150 students, dining facilities for those students, a college chapel to seat 200 to 250 students, a number of small lecture rooms, and one large lecture theatre to seat up to 200 students. For a university under desperate pressure for space and facilities, this sort of Anglican presence was exactly what the administration desired. In return, the college was not asked to surrender any teaching rights; it would proudly move on campus as an autonomous affiliated institution with its own academic program and its own students. The university at this time was contemplating the creation of a college system to be at the heart of arts and sciences at the institution. This would bring into being the earlier vision of the Carnegie Foundation's report of 1923, which called for colleges to provide primary communities to prevent students from becoming lost in the larger university. A new university college would be introduced, and all arts and sciences students were to become members of a college, in order to provide them with some institutional base beyond that of the various departments. The university generously offered to provide laboratory facilities for science courses, provided college enrolees paid the lab fees. The college would become the sole provider of teaching in religious studies, Oriental languages and literature, Hellenistic Greek, and Christian origins. As well, the college would be allowed to offer sections in most arts and sciences disciplines, or its own courses. The college library would remain in existence, but college students would have access to the main library at the university as well. A myriad of other details were left for further negotiation, but the main lines of the 1955 arrangement were clear, and plainly auspicious for St. John's.

The agreement with the university was taken to the college council on 9 May 1955. This meeting voted to set September 1958 as the target for the beginning of academic teaching at Fort Garry, and began to discuss ideas for the physical facility and the appointment of an architect to turn it into reality. A firm of fundraising consultants was proposed to prepare the way for a full-scale campaign. The meeting was informed that 243 members had joined the college convocation, plus eighty-two paid-up alumni, and nearly $5000 had been raised by this means. A subsequent "St. John's College Hey!Day" on 14 May was held in the Winnipeg Auditorium from 8:30 a.m. to midnight. It attracted a large crowd and raised over $5000 for the building fund. Peggy Sellers followed up the Hey!Day with a scheme based on the parable of the talents. Women in the women's auxiliaries of the church were encouraged to use their talents to raise money to help move the college. This "Talent Plan" raised another $20,000.

The new enthusiasm being generated for the college continued into the late spring of 1955, when it was briefly interrupted by a rumour circulating around the diocese. This rumour as reported to Warden Wilmot was that as soon as St. John's College was moved to the Fort Garry campus, the archbishop intended to shift all theological training in the prairie provinces to Emmanuel College, Saskatoon. The rumour seemed beyond belief, and, indeed, Archbishop Barfoot denied it vehemently.

Beginning with the 1955–56 academic year, St. John's College faced a number of exciting new challenges simultaneously. One was to fundraise for a new physical college on the Fort Garry campus. A second was to erect the new physical college. A third, and equally important, task was both to prepare the college's administration and academic staff for its new role on the campus and to take advantage of the financial funding being provided by the federal government, which was almost entirely tied to registrations. One of the real dangers was that the excitement of building a physical plant would detract from the more prosaic but equally important job of improving the infrastructure.

Fundraising and building (both new plant and infrastructure) all came together in an historic council meeting on 7 October 1955. This meeting named architects Moody and Moore to design the new Fort Garry college structure. It also heard from the fundraising consultants it had previously hired that the college should launch a major campaign for funds in the late spring of 1956. Planning was to begin in January 1956, with advanced gift-giving scheduled for 16 April to 12 May, intensive campaigning arranged from 14 May to 9 June, and a wrap-up until the end of June. These dates were scheduled remarkably soon after the final decision was taken, but some planning had been going on for months, and, moreover, life was generally simpler in 1955. The consultants thought a maximum of $700,000 could possibly be raised in the Winnipeg community, but suggested that $500,000 was a more realistic figure. At this same meeting, the chancellor recommended the creation of a dean of divinity, and told council that the dean and chapter of the cathedral had made $5000 available for the appointment of such a dean. This recommendation seemed sufficient answer to the earlier rumour that the chancellor was planning to move theology to Saskatoon.

From almost the very beginning, the fundraising campaign and the proposed cost of a new facility at Fort Garry were not quite in synchrony. The architect's plans for a college to accommodate 300 students with 100 in residence and an appropriate chapel would cost over a million dollars. As a result, council decided in the spring of 1957 to build only the educational building and the men's residence (with kitchen and dining facilities in the basement), with a tunnel to connect the two buildings. There would be no chapel, no women's residence, and no Great Hall. To keep costs down, the architects initially proposed a brick structure that many felt was out of keeping with the ambiance of the campus, but fortunately, a friend of the college offered a way to use Tyndall stone at virtually no increase in expense. Some, but not all, of the gap between what the college had been able to put into its capital fund and what was required by the buildings was met by construction grants from the federal government. The rest was borrowed from the banks. The actual construction was contracted to the firm of Wallace and Aikins Construction Company and the first sod was turned for the building on 2 May 1957 by the archbishop.

A day earlier, on 1 May 1957, the sixtieth session of the Synod of the Diocese of Rupert's Land had repealed the original statues of the college as amended in 1888, 1907, and 1932, replacing them with a new document. The statutes called for a college corporation, headed by the chancellor and including the major officers of the college. The corporation appointed the college council, which dealt with most business and academic matters of the college. In addition there was a college board, consisting of the warden and all faculty at the rank of associate professor or above, which dealt with academic discipline and academic standing, as well as recommendations for the appointment of fellows and for the award of scholarships and prizes. The fellows were obviously junior appointments, who "shall ordinarily reside in the College and take such teaching work as is assigned to them while engaged in research in the higher branches of their Department under the direction of the Professors in the Department in St. John's College or in the University of Manitoba."

By 1957, Warden Wilmot had succeeded in raising the registration to seventy-six undergraduates, fifteen students in theology, and three part-time students. Despite the isolation of the Broadway buildings, the college participated actively in intramural sports, with teams in 1956–57 getting to the finals in curling, basketball, and hockey, while the debating team won the Dingwall Trophy in 1957. *The Johnian* was actively published on a regular basis, and there was an annual yearbook, *The Black and Gold*. Wilmot had also employed the federal grant to good advantage, bringing in a number of bright young academics in the later 1950s and several first-rate senior people, of whom the best known was probably W.S.F. ("Bill") Pickering in sociology and anthropology. The warden worked hard to be certain that qualified professors of the college would be able to participate in the senior teaching of the university at honours and graduate levels, managing to negotiate several protocols with the university administration in this regard. Later, in the 1960s, the university was not so much offering college faculty access to upper-level teaching at the university, which had long been recognized, as it was threatening to withhold it.

For most of the period, before making a new appointment, the warden had to calculate carefully how the newcomer would be funded through increased registrations and grants. The system first came into question in 1957, when the archbishop as chancellor insisted on forcing through the appointment of a new dean of divinity (Dr. Wallace Wolverton, a graduate of the University of Chicago) over the warden's head without regard for finances. This appointment was probably the first example of tension between Warden Wilmot and Chancellor Barfoot. Up to this point, Wilmot had been generally allowed by the chancellor and the council to have his own way with appointments, and he had expected to be able to appoint Prof. Cecil Landon to the deanship. The warden and chancellor were able to present a united front in December 1957, however, when much debate occurred in council over the construction of the college chapel, deferred from the initial construction plans. The committee on building plans and construction wanted a multi-purpose chapel with sliding doors that could be enlarged to serve as a dining room and auditorium. Warden Wilmot and Chancellor Barfoot both agreed that a building solely "dedicated to the worship of Almighty God" was absolutely essential, and the architect was instructed by council to design a self-contained chapel.

Construction of the new building went relatively smoothly, and St. John's College was officially opened on 12 September 1958. The ceremony occurred just outside the entrance to the academic building. More than 1000 people were in attendance, most subsequently touring the new building. Two convocations were held that evening in the University Field House. The first was a special convocation for St. John's, and the second was a university event in which Chancellor Barfoot and Mr. A.E. Hoskins, now chancellor of the diocese, received honourary doctor of laws degrees. As it began a new life on the Fort Garry campus, the college had an enrolment of 152 students, nearly double its numbers in its last year on Broadway. A new golden age had—everyone hoped—finally begun.

The college moved to the former home of J.H. Ashdown in central Winnipeg at the corner of Hargrave and Broadway in 1945.

Expanding enrolment required the college to open a new women's residence at its Broadway site in 1954.

The crowded library (top) and chemistry classroom (below) of the Broadway building, c. 1955.

The college's hockey players in the residence, preparing for a game, c. 1955.

A billboard outside of the Women's Residence in 1955 advertises the college's fundraising drive for the move to the Fort Garry campus.

Rev. Canon Laurence Wilmot, warden from 1945 to 1960.

The 1955 fundraising drive included a "St. John's College Hey! Day," a day-long pep rally that included a parade through downtown Winnipeg led by the college cheerleaders.

The new college building at the Fort Garry campus (1959) with the chapel under construction.

The main office of the new Fort Garry building.

The college library c. 1958.

College students in the lounge (c. 1958), still wearing academic gowns.

Inside the new residence at the Fort Garry site.

Rev. Canon Cecil C. Landon, warden from 1961 to 1968.

Rev. Canon James R. Brown, warden from 1970 to 1980.

The college chapel shortly after its completion in 1959.

Premier (and later Governor-General) Ed Shreyer receives an honourary degree from the college in 1972. Shreyer had attended the college in the mid-1950s.

Rev. Canon Murdith McLean at his installation as warden in 1980.

Chapter Nine

On Campus, 1958–1970

THE FIRST TEN YEARS OF THE MOVE TO THE FORT GARRY CAMPUS were probably the best years that St. John's College ever experienced. This period came to a grinding halt in the later 1960s, terminated mainly by the federal government's decision to no longer give grants to individual educational institutions, but also by the decline of the post-war educational and religious booms. The result would be another serious threat to the continuation of the college. But for most of the 1960s, the college was an exciting place to be, even when it was briefly affected by internal dissension.

The St. John's College calendar for the 1958–59 academic year proudly announced that a "greater future" existed for it as an institution of higher education, now that it had moved to the university campus. Accommodation was in place for a student body of 300, including seventy-five residents (male only). A new growth in "academic stature" resulting from the move and new facilities would not mean any sacrifice in the advantages of a small college—"small classes and intimate association among staff and students." The college now had full access to the resources of the university, including specialized courses, library, and social and recreational services. The faculty of theology worked side by side with the faculty of arts and science, to their mutual advantage academically. The college was coeducational, the teaching staff was "appointed with a view both to Christian personality and to academic ability," and the "tone of the College" was "set by the daily chapel Services which all students are encouraged to attend." As the calendar noted, in 1958 St. John's was the "only one of the founding Colleges" to have taken up "its rightful place on the campus of the University of Manitoba." The college listed its faculty. The faculty of divinity had a dean, four members of professorial rank, and seven lecturers. A vacancy existed for the lecturer in ascetical theology. The faculty of arts and science also had a dean, and eighteen faculty members (ten of professorial rank) spread over ten departments: classics, English, Hellenistic Greek, history and political science, mathematics and science, modern languages, Oriental languages and literature, philosophy, religious studies, and sociology. There was no one in economics and one of the two positions in mathematics and science—at the instructor level—had not been filled at the time the calendar had gone to press.

The college had been brought—almost lured—to the Fort Garry campus by the vision of two successive university presidents and their administrations. This vision was of a university based squarely on the colleges, in which every student—at least in arts and science—belonged to a college and got his or her sense of identity from a college, some of which would have strong religious affiliations. The university would continue to have its faculties and academic departments, but those would be coequal with, if not indeed in many senses subordinated to, the colleges. Nobody ever tried to work out the administrative details of such an arrangement, which was just as well since they would have been almost as complicated as Canada itself. This vision was, in a very real sense, a fulfillment of the proposals made by W.S. Learned of the Carnegie Foundation as long ago as 1923, but it was untested. Apart from the possible administrative difficulties, the problems with the concept of a college-based university were, unfortunately, many. One resulted from the difficulty of successfully bringing all the founding colleges to Fort Garry. St. Paul's had joined St. John's on the campus in 1958, its building next door on Dysart Road. But the St. Boniface College and United College had no intention of moving to the suburbs, and hoped to achieve total administrative independence of the university. Another difficulty ensued from the weaknesses of the colleges in the sciences, which meant that vast areas of the curriculum were beyond their reach. Still another obstruction, particularly relevant to St. John's, was the softness of the religious underpinning of the institution. This softness manifested itself in two ways: first, the rapidity with which young Anglicans ceased to be concerned about their faith; and secondly, the external machinations of the Anglican authorities to remove theological education from St. John's College. Yet another element of disadvantage related to the dependence of the colleges on direct federal and provincial subsidy. Were that subsidy to be withdrawn, the colleges could be in serious financial difficulty.

But probably the most important obstacle to the great vision of the 1950s was the profound change the university had undergone in the latter years of that decade and would continue to undergo in the 1960s. The decade was one of enormous university expansion. Everywhere in Canada there existed a psychology of growth, with precious few concerned about what would happen if the conditions that fuelled growth ever disappeared. The world of higher education was especially susceptible, as in every province new universities and colleges were being constructed and old ones being expanded. St. John's College itself had shared in the growth, its own move to the campus fuelled by the expansion. The changes were not merely about size and scope. Everywhere the old ways were being cast aside and replaced by new ones supposedly more appropriate to the second half of the twentieth century. In terms of the University of Manitoba, this meant the complete acceptance of international academic standards, with their emphasis on disciplines, research, graduate degrees, professional training, centralization, and faculty organizations, as well as on tenure and academic freedom. What happened as a result of the new standards, of course, was that increasing numbers of faculty and administrators within the university did not buy into the college system, and even those within it could see advantages beyond the "community of colleges."

An indication of the way the academic wind was blowing came only a year after St. John's had opened its doors on the Fort Garry campus. On 13 October 1959, Prof. Meredith Jones, chairman of the faculty of arts building committee, reported that the committee was recommending creation of a new college (subsequently named University College) to accommodate a total of 750 students, 250 of whom would be housed in its own residence. At first glance it appeared that the administration's vision of the college system was being advanced. Actually, it was not. After much controversy, the academic committee had agreed that the new college would not be autonomous. It would not have its own faculty or its own curriculum, and therefore would not be like St. John's or St. Paul's (as they were at the time). It would instead be under the jurisdiction of the dean of arts, and would have to form its own society and community without a distinctive staff, curriculum, or chapel. This report of the arts building committee was debated at two special meetings of faculty council held in October. The faculty was evenly divided between those in favour of the committee's recommendation and those opposed. Those opposed naturally divided into those who thought the recommendation went too far and those who thought it did not go far enough. In the end, the dean of arts had to cast the deciding vote to proceed, and was able to do so only because one professor who was opposed had retired to his office during the vote. Whether a college could be made viable, which was not autonomous and which would have neither its own staff nor its own teaching program, was another matter entirely. The "University College model" was certainly not, in the long run, congenial to the college system at the University of Manitoba.

The first year on the campus saw continued physical expansion of St. John's College. The first tenders for the construction of the chapel, opened by the building committee in the summer of 1958, were a shock, running well in excess of the $200,000 that had been planned for the building. The plans had to be scaled down, and Tyndall stone introduced, in order to get the tenders within the limits. But there seemed no doubt that a chapel was desperately needed, since the temporary chapel, holding ninety persons, was full every morning during the time slot in the university timetable set aside for chapel and other such meetings. Warden Wilmot turned the first soil for the new chapel on an extremely cold January day in 1959, using a bulldozer. In the spring of 1959 the college council also authorized the construction of a new wing of the residence, intended to accommodate women. This wing also cost $200,000, and its construction was greatly facilitated by a new provincial formula for capital grants that provided 25 percent of construction costs. Finally, the council authorized the construction of two small science laboratories in the basement of the main building, designed to accommodate thirty-two places in chemistry and thirty-two in physics (although not simultaneously). This would make possible self-contained instruction in first-year science for the first time. On the teaching staff front, the council in 1958 approved a pension plan for the faculty in association with Great-West Life. A number of new appointments were made early in 1959, including those of A.M.C. Waterman and George Baldwin—both still fellows in 2006—as part-time instructors in economics and science, respectively.

The college authorities, led by Warden Wilmot, were quite energetic in the spring of 1959 in recruiting and publicizing the college in the Anglican community. Wilmot made a lengthy visit to high schools in northern Manitoba, and others visited schools in Winnipeg and the southern agricultural areas. The rural regions were informed of the residential accommodation for both men and women for the 1959 academic year. The result of the heavy recruiting was another spike in college enrolment for the 1959–60 academic year. The total was 248 students, including sixteen in theological programs and a number in graduate studies. There were forty-six women in the new residence. Despite the increase in numbers, however, the college was still running a deficit of $8000 to $10,000 a year in its operating budget, as it had done throughout the 1950s, and it was still making up the shortfall by collecting dribs and drabs of donations from the Anglican business community.

On the negative side, tension seemed to be increasing between the college and its chancellor, also the archbishop of the diocese and the Primate of All Canada. We know about this only because of Laurie Wilmot's extraordinarily frank memoir; understandably, nothing can be found on the early background of this matter in the official college records. Wilmot claimed that neither he nor anyone else could understand the nature of the problem, particularly regarding the chancellor's interventions in the treatment of individual students by the divinity school and faculty, but in retrospect the pattern seems plain enough. In an aside to the diocesan synod, Chancellor Barfoot once confessed that he found the course offerings of the divinity faculty of the college better suited to the University of Chicago than to a small institution on the Canadian prairies training parish priests. He had objected when divinity faculty were to be paid on the same scale as secular faculty instead of on the scale of diocesan clergy. The warden had argued that the faculty was entitled to extra pay for its extra years and training and acquired academic credentials. Herein exactly was the problem. From Barfoot's perspective, the divinity school had become too academic and had lost contact with the world of the parishes.

That the divinity faculty had become more academic was not surprising. Virtually all the academic programs of the university over which the college had a monopoly and did not have to fit into the arrangements of others— religious studies, Oriental languages and literature, Hellenistic Greek, and Christian origins—were divinity ones, at least in origin. To the extent that these were the programs that were strengthened in the later 1950s, especially after the arrival of Dean Wallace Wolverton from the University of Chicago, the college was taking a path away from the parishes and ordinary parish priests. The faculty of divinity under Wolverton had replaced the old licentiate of theology with a new program leading to a degree of bachelor of theology and introduced graduate work as well. In the nineteenth century it had been possible to allow divinity to be taught by men who specialized in the recondite fields of the old languages. Even if early parishioners did not often speak Greek or Hebrew, they understood the value of the old learning. By the mid-twentieth century, however, such "esoteric" fields had clearly been consigned to the academy.

The nature of the controversy sharpened at a meeting of college council on 17 February 1960 devoted to staffing matters. Initially at issue was an appointment in systematic theology in the divinity school. If Prof. Landon were to develop courses in philosophy at the college, he could no longer cover this crucial area in theology as he had done for several years past. The archbishop interjected at this point that he thought "systematics" absolutely essential to theology. He then went on to offer his opinion that the college was overloaded in the fields of Oriental languages and literature and in Old Testament—the academic areas the divinity school was presently developing. Warden Wilmot bristled. He wrote in his memoir that the archbishop should have reached that decision five or six years earlier—and Barfoot should have said so at the time. Instead, Barfoot had insisted on beefing up Old Testament and on the appointment of Prof. Wolverton as dean and professor in 1956. Wolverton had come in and had successfully developed Old Testament as a serious academic enterprise. This was, of course, precisely the problem from Archbishop Barfoot's perspective. The college was offering courses that belonged to a university, at the graduate level even, rather than to an undergraduate school of theology catering to ordinary parish priests. Wilmot responded that the Old Testament courses were very popular with students outside the college, helping to bring in revenue to support a theological school of only fifteen to twenty students. Unspoken here was the assumption that the theological school on its own was no longer pulling its weight. Barfoot in turn insisted that the college had lost sight of its mission to teach undergraduate theology and to prepare parish priests.

The controversy on one level was part of the teething pains of reinvigorating St. John's as an academic institution on the Fort Garry campus. Part of Warden Wilmot's grievance was that the man Barfoot was now attacking was the man Barfoot had personally appointed. But clearly the archbishop had not expected Wallace Wolverton to move so quickly and so successfully in an academic direction, probably because Barfoot did not himself understand how the academy had changed since the 1930s. For his part, Warden Wilmot did not seem to understand that in one important sense Barfoot was right. St. John's College could not turn itself into a high-powered academic institution while maintaining in its divinity school an undergraduate program principally intended to train parish priests for a diocese that no longer revered learning for its own sake.

At the same time, the chancellor was not prepared to allow St. John's to transform itself into a secular liberal arts college. At the close of the council meeting of 17 February, almost as an afterthought, the archbishop moved the appointment of Dr. Alexander Hull as associate professor of modern languages and head of the department. Hull was an American presently teaching at the University of Massachusetts, but he was married to a Canadian and one of his three books was a study of the French-Canadian dialect. When his appointment had been earlier discussed in committee, the archbishop had queried whether he was a member of the Anglican Church and was told that he had been married in an Anglican Church. To the motion of Hull's appointment earlier introduced by the warden, Barfoot added the phrase that he was a member of the Anglican Church. Thus began the Hull saga, which split the college at the very opening of the new decade and close to the beginning of what should have been the college's great new era. Archbishop Barfoot had already made clear to council that he felt that all faculty and staff of the college should be Anglicans, in accordance with the constitution of the college, which stated that "the teaching and government of the College should always be in conformity with the Discipline and Doctrine of the Church of England." Such a requirement was common in sectarian institutions in the nineteenth and earlier twentieth centuries, and was certainly fulfilled when the faculty were clergymen, but was becoming increasingly anachronistic in the new world of the academy in the second half of the twentieth century. Warden Wilmot and others had attempted to talk Barfoot out of this position, insisting that such a requirement would reduce St. John's College to sectarian status and was probably illegal, as well.

The resulting power struggle between chancellor and warden has been detailed, from the warden's perspective, in Laurie Wilmot's memoir. To summarize later developments, the dean of St. John's College (John Matthews) had learned in discussions with Prof. Hull that he was not an Anglican, but sometimes attended a Unitarian Church. The Unitarians, of course, were not accepted as Christians by the World Council of Churches. When informed of this fact, the archbishop tried to force each clerical member of faculty to declare his position on the issue in writing. Fearing another version of the recent Crowe affair at United College—where academic freedom had been infringed by a clumsy clerical president—the faculty refused. At a meeting of the college board without the archbishop being present, the warden reported that he had checked with three other Anglican educational institutions in Canada on this question. All appointed non-Anglicans, and all but Bishop's University would in theory appoint a non-Christian. None of these institutions was sympathetic to a denominational test for faculty. The board reaffirmed unanimously the appointment of Alexander Hull. Warden Wilmot, at the chancellor's request, prepared a statement for the next meeting of council, rehearsing the situation. Wilmot acknowledged that appointments to the faculty of arts and science should normally be Anglicans, but that given academic considerations, the appointment of a non-Christian might be acceptable.

The showdown came at a special meeting of college council held at St. George's Church, Crescentwood, on Saturday, 23 April 1960. The meeting decided that the appointment could not be rescinded, as the archbishop had initially requested. Barfoot eventually accepted this conclusion, but he added that since the warden had been wilfully ecclesiastically disobedient, he would be placed on probation for a year if he did not apologize and accept full responsibility for the situation he had created. Wilmot refused to apologize, and he was slowly but inexorably forced into a position where he would have to retire from the wardenship. He managed to outstay the chancellor, who resigned effective 31 December 1960. Wilmot stepped down at the close of the 1960–61 academic year. Convinced his clerical reputation had been greatly damaged, Wilmot left Winnipeg and the diocese of Rupert's Land for some years. He returned to the diocese in 1972 and, after retirement in 1977, came back to the college as an elder statesman.

In retrospect, the contretemps between Warden Wilmot and Archbishop Barfoot seems far more than a personal power struggle between two strong personalities. Lurking in the background was the whole question of the viability of denominational education, in Manitoba and in Canada as a whole, particularly with increasing levels of public funding. Given the rapidity of secularization, by the time ex-warden Wilmot reappeared at St. John's College in the later 1970s, the 1960 controversy would seem something to have come straight from the nineteenth century, so quickly had times changed.

Despite the furor in the spring of 1960, associated with leaked reports of the disciplinary action taken against Warden Wilmot, and the subsequent departures of most of the principals (Wolverton and Barfoot in 1960, Wilmot in 1961, and Matthews in 1962), life at the college went on. After a year as acting warden, Dr. Cecil C. Landon became warden in 1962. Blake Wood became dean of divinity. From a student's (and faculty member's) perspective, indeed, the first half of the 1960s was in many ways a golden era for the college. It was much larger than it had ever been before, both in terms of faculty and student body. Faculty, which had organized into a faculty association, were admitted onto the college council and were thus part of the decision-making process. The college was independent, with its own registrar and its own registration for courses, but its students were allowed to participate in all campus activities on an equal basis with all other university students. The college was certainly able to maintain its distinctiveness, as was documented by a 1964 study of religious life among university undergraduates headed by William Pickering. By the mid-1960s, two-thirds of St. John's students were Anglican, although only 6 percent attended religious services in the chapel. (In 1968 Anthony Waterman asserted that chapel attendance averaged about six on weekdays and a dozen on Sundays, while only one lay member of faculty attended chapel and most faculty "have no recognizable religious profession.") Fully three-quarters of the student members of the college were of British background. Despite the residence, a high percentage of Johnians lived at home because so many Anglicans were urban residents. Anglican students at the university were among the most likely of all students at the university to change their devotional habits in a negative direction. They showed a considerable "resistance to the teaching of their church on socio-religious issues." Students not at St. John's often reacted negatively to the clannishness and "snootiness" of the college, and the student leadership at the college itself often complained of this as well. At one point in 1966, the senior stick at University College commented on "the minor nonconformists and members of the 'River Heights culture'" that made up St. John's College.

Among the major student issues of the period was the desire for the construction of a Great Hall (raised by political studies professor Wally Fox-Decent in 1963). The student newspaper *The Belch* in 1964 went so far as to suggest that the college—which it claimed had "no clear cut vision or goal"—would close without the building of a Great Hall and other new facilities, including a theatre and a faculty lounge. College council in the mid-1960s, however, most of the time was less interested in more buildings than it was in balancing the books. The dictum of Charles Dickens's character Mr. Micawber still applied. A favourable balance in annual income meant happiness; an unfavourable one meant misery. St. John's College was annually miserable. According to a study done by the university, part of the problem was that the cost of educating a single student was 40 percent higher at St. John's, chiefly because all classes were not fully enrolled and there were few economies of scale.

Revenue came from a variety of sources, and was limited in a variety of ways. Tuition fees were one source of revenue, but the university controlled the amount of tuition that could be charged; St. John's could not greatly exceed university fees and expect to survive. In the academic year 1966–67 the college got one-third of its revenue from tuition and fees and another 23 percent from residence charges (room and board). The college budget of the time does not allow for the computation of the profit and loss of the residence and food services, but clearly the college lost money on these items. That the budget did not attempt to balance revenue from room and board and the costs of room and board speaks for itself. Grants, mainly federal, were another source of revenue. In 1966–67 the college received 30 percent of its income from grants (federal and provincial). The granting formula was important. A pencilled note in the college archives on one proposed national grant increase observed that the formula would increase the college's income by almost $30,000 a year. Unfortunately, this increase was never implemented and instead the granting mechanism was subsequently altered to the college's disadvantage. Revenue could also come from gifts, endowment, and the diocese. But St. John's had never recovered its endowment base after the defalcation, and it still did not have a fundraising officer, much less a full-time one. The college got only 3 percent of its revenue from endowment, a miniscule proportion, given the age and venerability of the institution. Most of the "experts" held that the diocese had been "funded out" by the building campaign of the 1950s and were fearful of chancing another drive. Thus, the arrival of the college centennial in 1966 was not accompanied by a fundraising campaign of any sort. Less than 1 percent of revenue came from the diocese. The operating deficit for 1966–67 was $102,000, the accumulated deficit as of 30 June 1967 was $369,269, and over $200,000 in bank loans (mainly for the buildings of 1959–60) was still owing.

In the meantime, most students could be found in the canteen underneath the chapel, along with the faculty, drinking coffee, socializing, and generally making a mess. Student culture underwent a major transformation in the 1960s, part of a general emancipation of manners and morals in which the traditional values of the nation's Victorian ancestors were overturned virtually overnight. But firmly held beliefs do not collapse as rapidly as the developments of the decade might suggest. Rather, a moral system of behaviour that was already in a state of deterioration, and was out of step with what people actually did and said in their daily lives, proved incapable of surviving widespread scrutiny. In any case, the results for St. John's students were obvious. One was in dress. Until the mid-1960s, male students wore shirts, ties, and jackets to university, while female students wore blouses and skirts. At St. John's, academic gowns had traditionally been worn over this garb. Now suddenly both sexes appeared in sweatshirts, jeans, and running shoes. Student language became increasingly laced with vulgarities and swearwords, and sex ceased to be a verboten subject for public discussion. Students now talked and wrote openly about sexual intercourse, contraception, abortion, premarital sex, drugs, and homosexuality. They smoked and drank equally openly. Students were increasingly untidy and they ceased to attend chapel. The student council actually closed the canteen for a week in 1966, and the student newspaper of the time (appropriately named *The Belch*, with a single-page addendum after 1964 called *The Burp*) noted, "Stick heard to say choice words about lack of notices exhorting cleanliness and the effect on first year students. 'How were they supposed to know they weren't supposed to keep crap off the tables?'" The wearing of gowns became a major issue in 1964, when a referendum was held on the question. The vote decided to keep the gowns, and students wore them for a time, but usage soon fell off again.

Student leaders constantly complained about apathy, the non-wearing of gowns, the dirt and untidiness of student facilities, the decline of attendance at chapel, and the decline in participation in Commemoration beyond the ball (eventually only the choir went). *The Belch* in 1964 produced a *St. John's College Colouring Book*, with imaginary pictures and captions. One caption on the Women's Common Room noted "there are many bodies 'hung over' the furniture. There are many books placed all over the floor. Under the books are cigarette butts. Under the cigarette butts is dirt. Colour it casual." The chapel's annotation was: "This is the Chapel. There are services here everyday. Everybody loves to go to Chapel. Colour it empty." At the start of the 1960s the Commem Ball, at least, was well attended and enjoyed by students and faculty alike. The student newspaper in 1962 reported that Murdith McLean, Dr. Pickering, and Professor Waterman had all been seen in "high spirits" cavorting there. But by 1970 student dances were a dying activity. Student "high jinks" of various sorts were common earlier in the decade. In 1964 a panty raid occurred in the res. The various items involved were collected up the following day. The college was always active and competitive in intramural sports. Many teams from the college were unofficially called "the Montcalm Maulers," reflecting the name of the closest watering hole to the campus. For three years in the early sixties, 1962 to 1964, houses (Anderson, West, Machray, and Matheson, all named after important figures in the institution's history) were formed for internal intramural competition, but the innovation did not last. Debating rose and fell back again. St. John's followed most of the fads and fashions of the 1960s, including a bout of anti-Americanism. *The Belch* on 31 October 1966 had only one line on its front page: "Yankee Capital Go Home!" All in all, Johnians were engaged in college life but were not "rah-rah" about it, especially before 1968. For several years after that date, students were demoralized.

Regardless of the student alarmism of 1964, the college in the mid-1960s certainly had no real warning of the funding and administrative crisis about to confront it. In 1964 St. John's College applied to become a member of the National Conference of Canadian Universities and Colleges (NCCUC), an organization devoted in large measure to lobbying for increased federal grants for higher education. In 1966 the NCCUC would become the Association of Universities and Colleges of Canada. As a result of a favourable report by a visiting committee of academics, the college was invited to send observers to the 1964 annual meeting of the NCCUC, at which its membership application was successfully approved. St. John's had become a full-fledged Canadian institution of higher learning. By this time, however, the days in which the college's administrators would receive numbers-driven financial grants from the federal government were clearly coming to an end. Several Dominion-wide committees investigated university financing (the Bladen Committee) and the administration of Canadian universities (the

Duff-Berdahl Commission). As a member of the NCCUC, the college was able to provide autonomous financial statistics for the Commission on the Financing of Higher Education that produced the Bladen report.

The province of Manitoba clearly wanted decisions about higher education made in a different manner from the past, and it wanted much more control over funding. In the short run, Manitoba established a seven-member Council of Higher Learning, which would permit recommendations on policy to be made outside the corridors of power in the legislature. The province also cooperated with other provinces in attempting to pressure the federal government to end its granting system, part of a general tendency toward the assertion of provincial rights during the period. The Council of Higher Learning moved over the course of the year 1966 to propose major changes to the university system in the province, most of them connected with the colleges. The college situation had been the cause of much discontent for years, of course. Brandon and United colleges, and to some extent St. Boniface College, chafed under University of Manitoba tutelage. For their part, administrators at the University of Manitoba, led by William Sibley, the dean of the faculty of arts and science, chafed at the autonomy of the affiliated colleges on the Fort Garry campus. Sibley insisted that the colleges made it impossible to conduct rational academic planning, claiming that what was needed was "one Board, one President, one Dean, one Department head." St. John's and St. Paul's were extremely worried about finances, particularly given their continual deficits and the threat and ultimate announcement of the termination of federal per capita grants. The Council of Higher Learning responded to the unrest by proposing to detach Brandon and United colleges as separate universities, to continue St. Boniface as a teaching centre in French, and to produce a new closer relationship with the University of Manitoba for St. John's and St. Paul's, probably along the lines of that already prevailing at University College. The new order on the Fort Garry campus would be determined by a special committee on college structure, chaired by Lionel Funt, of the mathematics department, which would deliberate on the matter in the spring of 1967.

In October 1966, on virtually the same day that St. John's College began the formal celebration of the centennial of its founding, the federal government announced that it would change its funding policies for higher education. In place of a direct per capita student grant to each institution, federal aid would take the form of block grants to the provincial governments. This alteration would place the responsibility for higher education almost completely in the hands of the province and would devastate the college's funding. The first college event of St. John's celebration was a birthday dance in the Students' Union Building, followed by a formal dinner held at the Fort Garry Hotel on Friday, 28 October 1966, in the presence of the Most Reverend H.H. Clark, Primate of All Canada. The menu was seafood cocktail, cream of mushroom soup, roast turkey with cranberry sauce, buttered green beans, and crême de menthe parfait. *La plus ça change*. L.R. ("Bud") Sherman, MP, gave the after-dinner address, and a dance followed. A report of the centennial celebrations in the *Winnipeg Tribune* spoke of the troubles faced in the past by the college, but did not suggest that survival was problematic. The newspaper piece closed with a quotation allegedly by Sidney Smith, formerly president of the University of Manitoba, to the effect that "At St. John's the fine old-fashioned epithet 'a gentleman and a scholar' has been and is . . . the most coveted title." The 100th annual convocation of the college was held on Tuesday, 1 November. The convocation address was given by Old Boy Arnold Heeney, one of the college's Rhodes Scholars and most recently clerk of the federal Privy Council, who was awarded a doctor of canon laws. H.H. Clark, archbishop of Rupert's Land, chancellor of the college, and recently appointed Primate of All Canada, also received an honourary doctor of laws.

Other events of the centennial included an historical revue staged by the students, a lecture series by college faculty, a special chamber music concert early in 1967, and the publication of Bill Fraser's history of the college. Wally Fox-Decent, by now executive assistant to Premier Duff Roblin, did his best to encourage the CBC to make St. John's College the topic for the national television program *Heritage*, but without success. A memorandum from the chairman of the college centennial committee, W.A. Harshaw, complained in September 1966 that little publicity work had been done for the occasion, especially outside the college itself. Here was an opportunity to stake the historic claim of the college within the larger community, or to begin a fundraising campaign, but it was passed over by default. The college archives do contain some receipts for publicity expenses incurred by the college in September 1966 in promoting the centennial. A meeting with a reporter from the *Free Press* produced a bill from the Ivanhoe Cabaret for $2.40, and a man from the cbc was entertained at the Fort Garry Lounge to the tune of $4.00.

While the university committee on college structure met regularly in the spring of 1967, so did the diocesan council. As a result, the provincial synod of the diocese of Rupert's Land at its meeting on 23–24 May 1967 voted to recognize the College of Emmanuel St. Chad in Saskatoon as the theological college for the diocese and the recipient of all grants for theological education. St. John's College was recognized as "the Liberal Arts and Science College for the Province [of Rupert's Land]." Thus, in the end, Bishop Barfoot won the battle with Warden Wilmot. A memorandum on this synod's actions to be found in the college archives notes, "we were given to understand that St. John's College representative on the Provincial Committee had concurred in this." Perhaps the delegate was so stunned by the action that he put up no resistance. Alternatively, it is possible that the college was not very concerned about the decision. At the same time that the synod had recognized St. Chad's, it also allowed Archbishop Clark as Primate of All Canada to move to Toronto to be closer to the national action. His voice was thus effectively lost as the funding crisis loomed more apparent.

Warden Landon argued in a piece for the September 1967 *Rupert's Land News* that the synod's action was merely to recognize "only one institution for training ordinands in the Province of Rupert's Land" and did not affect most aspects of theological education at St. John's. By this time Cecil Landon was visibly weakened by the cancer that would shortly end his life, and was not at his best in responding to the flurry of blows raining down on the college. Landon emphasized that the college still had responsibility for pre-theological education, for post-graduate work in theology, for the academy of religion for the laity, and for its share of staffing of the religious studies department of the University of Manitoba. "So then," he concluded, "there is no death of Theology—nor of God—at St. John's." What had died was not God but the diocesan funding and, shortly thereafter, with the departure of the dean of theology, the faculty of theology itself.

As for the committee on college structure, its final report addressed the questions of programs of studies, the status of teaching staffs, and the working relationships between colleges and their individual departments. Although never mentioned by name, the University College model was the one recommended by the committee. The recommendations of the committee did not elaborate the details of operation, but established what Warden Landon told synod were "basic principles upon which a community of Colleges on the Fort Garry campus might be established." The colleges would have their courses, their faculties, and their libraries integrated into those of the university, would be encouraged to maintain certain areas of "emphasis and excellence" in a balanced program, and would be autonomous mainly in a social sense. Few faculty could be found who were willing to gamble their futures on a college appointment over the long haul, particularly given the alternative. Faculty members would not have their rank reduced or their tenure affected when they became full members of university departments, and they would become eligible for graduate and honours supervision within their new departments. In return for their surrender of autonomy, the colleges would receive the provision of "ancillary services" from the university. As Warden Landon noted to synod, the Funt Report resulted from full negotiations with the university, the Council on Higher Learning, and the Minister of Education, and was unanimously accepted in principle by all governing bodies, including the council of St. John's College. It was clear that the demoralized college council felt that it had no little real choice. The diocese had pulled the plug on the training of ordinands (and the diocesan grant) at St. John's, and the federal government had pulled the plug on separate funding for the colleges. The university administration had not orchestrated the many blows received by St. John's in 1967, but it was prepared to take advantage of them in the name of administrative efficiency. The college responded on 7 June 1967 by accepting the principles of the Funt Report.

As University of Manitoba President Hugh H. Saunderson pointed out in late 1967 in a personal letter to Desmond Smith (one of the college's representatives on the Funt committee), the chief consideration behind the acceptance of Funt had been that "unless your costs are joined in with ours along the line suggested, the financial support from government, if it is to be reasonably equitable, will not be enough to keep St. John's solvent." In this letter, Saunderson was quite brutal about the implications of the college's decision. Apparently Warden Landon did not fully understand or accept what the college had agreed to, and was still hoping to maintain some vestige of autonomy, symbolized by the preservation of a college dean of faculty. The notion of a college dean was absurd, scoffed Saunderson. "There will have to be one Faculty of Arts and Science," and one chain of command; he would not allow anything else. Administrative officers within the college paralleling the university administration were also to be limited, since they were no longer needed. "Members of the departments . . . will be, by mutual agreement, in various institutions as a locational base, and will contribute to the 'ethos' of the College where they are located. We certainly find this to be the case in University College, where the 'ethos' or 'spirit' is certainly markedly different from that found in the science buildings or in Tier." So much for the vision of a community of colleges that Saunderson had presented to the St. John's College when he had invited it to the Fort Garry campus some years earlier. Ironically, Saunderson still talked about the "community of colleges," but by 1967 this meant little more than the maintenance of the names of the buildings. Having swallowed the bait whole at the outset, St. John's and St. Paul's would now spend several years trying to wriggle off the hook.

On 1 July 1967, the University Grants Commission (UGC) succeeded the Council on Higher Learning, with, among other responsibilities, a mandate to administer the block grant Manitoba would now receive from the Dominion. It was not clear at the beginning whether the UGC would continue a direct per capita granting system or would go to an omnibus budget for the university. The university wanted the colleges to submit budgets to it in August 1967, but the colleges decided to submit their financial requests directly to the UGC instead. A compromise eventually was worked out whereby the university assumed responsibility for the academic budget of the colleges and the colleges' budget requests became part of the university one.

St. John's College expressed many criticisms and reservations of the Funt Report. Dean Sibley in October 1967 wrote the chairman of the college council that it was clear that the college was "unable to accept the admittedly serious limitation on its traditional autonomy" entailed by Funt, and was certainly entitled to go its own way. As he well knew, an independent course was impossible without the external funding that had been withdrawn. Thus in the winter of 1967–68 the college became involved in discussions initiated by President Saunderson regarding the so-called "Community of Colleges," clearly intended to prepare the ground for a much less autonomous new relationship between the university and its colleges. At these meetings St. John's attempted to maintain some power over academic appointments, partly in anticipation of the revival of a faculty of theology and partly "in case of a future separation of the College and the University." The college's position was that the "agreement with the university must be framed so that it does not close the door to future development of the College." This qualification was waved away by the university administration, and the University Grants Commission insisted that there would have to be a signed agreement in place between the colleges and the university before 1 April 1968 in order to make any allocation of funds for the continual support of both St. John's and St. Paul's.

In March 1968 the college signed a letter of agreement with the university. This letter acknowledged that while the college accepted the principles of the Funt Report, "a period of experimentation will be required to develop the unpredictable situations and problems which are bound to evolve and which will have to be settled or solved on an ad hoc basis as they arise." The letter of intent added, "it would not be prudent to attempt now the preparation of a final agreement which would provide for the handling of circumstances not yet in contemplation, but after a trial period of one year or longer (as may be decided) it should be possible to reduce to final form the agreement which would govern the future relationship between the Colleges and the University." By this time Cecil Landon was dead and Blake Wood had become acting warden.

There were a number of unsettled issues between the college and the university, some of which were identified by St. John's College Dean of Studies David Lawless in a memorandum dated 13 December 1968. Lawless called attention to three points. First, there was no clear understanding of the relationship of the college library to the university library. Secondly, there was no agreement on the so-called "areas of emphasis and supported areas" mentioned in the Funt Report. Lawless added, "The question of areas of emphasis and excellence is not as clear cut as it may first appear." The problem was partly that the department heads in arts and science, who controlled teaching, would have to consent to any college area of excellence. This constraint worked against most good ideas for areas of emphasis. Finally, wrote Lawless, the number of students to be located at the college depended on the measurement of "a student." If students meant bodies, the college was close to achieving its own expressed goal. (Indeed, according to one loose set of registration figures in the college papers for October 1969, over 2100 students were enrolled in the college in fifty-six classes representing fourteen disciplines, with English, history, and psychology being the most numerous.) If students meant full-time equivalents, with each class enrolment representing one-fifth of a full-time student, there were only about 400 in the college. An earlier letter from Dean William Sibley to President Saunderson had suggested another issue. Sibley, on behalf of his faculty, expressed opposition to the granting of tenure in the colleges to any faculty member during the period of "experimentation." Career paths would be on hold until the colleges came to terms.

While some were attempting to sort out, without much success, the practical details of the proposed arrangement with the university, Anthony Waterman—president of the St. John's College Faculty Association—attempted in a memorandum dated 14 May 1968 to look at the larger question of the future of St. John's College. He pointed out that there were two British models of a college, one an older mediaeval version and another that was basically "a university in microcosm." He then asked, "what kind of college is St. John's?" answering that the college had always been too poor to be a successful university college and too uncertain of its purpose to be a true mediaeval one. Fortunately, the proposed agreement had wiped the slate clean, "and we are ready to start again, remarkably unembarrassed by any legacy of tradition." While there were no constraints from the past, there were obviously some limits flowing from the agreement, including the full integration of formal instruction into the university system. Nevertheless, Waterman proposed that certain academics housed at the college be invited to become tutors, supervising the general programs of selected students. This was a concept that could have been taken more seriously, but apparently was not pursued at the time. Despite the pessimism of this memorandum, two months earlier Waterman had submitted a brief to the University Grants Commission on behalf of the St. John's College Faculty Association that argued for the preservation of "a certain number of small and anomalous enclaves within the educational system" by allowing the colleges "far more freedom than is presently thought proper," presumably by the university.

If the Waterman plea for "anomalous enclaves" may have represented the position of many college faculty toward the university, a student cluster called "the Group" held a teach-in in February 1968 and several subsequent meetings to discuss "the future of the college." As their issue of first importance, the students strongly opposed the introduction of television lectures into the college. They also felt that there was precious little college feeling abroad, at least in 1968. The common room "was not exactly a hot bed of debate" and few student activities were well supported. The students adjourned their discussions because of the proximity of final examinations, and they were never resumed. Much discussion occurred in the college over the future in the period between 1968 and the signing of the final agreement in 1970, and a number of important decisions were made that would influence the life of the college after the completion of the agreement in 1970.

One of the most important of these decisions revolved around the question of the relationship between the college and those faculty members housed within it. It must be remembered that the post-agreement college would be virtually without precedent in North American higher education, for its faculty would be paid by the university and completely directed in their teaching responsibilities by their departments. How much choice of membership this left the college was an interesting matter. According to the Funt Report and the interim agreement, faculty had to be willing to be housed in or teach in St. John's College. A meeting of college council on 5 March 1969 accepted in principle a draft letter of college appointment that stated that appointments to the college would come either from applicants named by the college and accepted by the university, or from consenting members of the university faculty. The letter stressed that "the College has the right to appoint faculty to membership in the College." It was left unstated that the right to appoint faculty was not exclusively the college's. The council made a distinction between those appointed to teach in the college (they were members) and those merely housed in the college to accommodate the department or those teaching only one course or section (they were not members). Some members of council wanted the letter to spell out privileges of membership further, and the draft of a new letter was authorized.

Another important question concerned the appointment of a new warden. No strong internal candidate appeared, and so the college council searched outside. It managed to find a suitable candidate within Canada, but in the final stages of negotiations he decided against accepting the position. In the end, council recommended the Reverend James Brown, a Canadian who had been teaching at Nashotah House, an Episcopal Church seminary in Nashotah, Wisconsin. Before making the appointment, the college asked President Saunderson for an assurance that Brown would be able to teach a course in the department of religion. The chair of religion replied that he would need to examine credentials before this could happen, and in a letter dated 24 November 1969 President Saunderson pointed out that he had not been invited to meet with Brown when he had been interviewed for the post, adding "I am naturally reluctant to recommend to the Board, for formal appointment, any senior staff person without any personal knowledge of him or her." Acting warden Blake Wood responded that the college still had the right to appoint its own head, and only needed to inform the board, but Saunderson emphasized that the line item paying the warden's salary was in the administration's budget. In the end, the college filled out a President's Form number 1—the university's appointment form—and the appointment was officially approved by the university's board of governors. Brown eventually taught his course on an annual ad hoc basis.

In his Dean of Studies Report in October 1969, David Lawless reported on several recent decisions by the faculty of arts that would have an effect on St. John's College. One was an approval in principle that a program be initiated in Canadian studies, to be centred in St. John's. Another was a faculty of arts recommendation to senate and the university's board of governors that additional space be created at the college, so that up to fifty-five instructors could be accommodated with suitable new classroom space and student facilities. This would, early in 1970, lead to a university decision to build a new wing to the college.

The final agreements between St. John's College and St. Paul's College and the University of Manitoba were executed on 11 June 1970. The preamble noted the arrangement of March 1968 and stated that "the terms of the Arrangement have governed the relationship between the University and the Colleges since April 1, 1968." This arrangement was formally continued in the agreement. No major concessions had been won by the colleges during the "period of experimentation." Neither arrangement nor agreement was substantially different from the recommendations of the Funt Report, and the Funt "basic principles" were to be applied in all matters affecting the relationship between the colleges and the university that were not specifically spelled out in the agreement. College faculty as of 1 April 1968 were appointed to university staff at a salary no less than that paid by the college on 31 December 1967, and the university was given the power to "assign to each College . . . such academic staff suitably distributed as to academic ranks, as may from time to time be reasonably required to conduct the academic programme in the College to the same standard as is maintained by the University in similar courses conducted in its own buildings." The library arrangement was still not spelled out in any detail, although the Funt Report had stated as a principle that "provision should be made for the continuation of the college libraries and for the maintaining within each college of suitable collections of current material at the undergraduate level, pertinent to the areas of emphasis of the college."

The "areas of emphasis" in either college's academic program were not actually specified. Surviving documentation suggests that what many in the university had in mind for "areas of emphasis" for St. John's were esoteric subjects like Greek and Hebrew already taught by the college, although Lionel Funt (chairman of the committee on college structure) in 1968 had privately insisted that there should be "some central thread of continuity in the College's academic program." Elaborating on his view of the "areas of excellence" concept, Funt suggested concentration on a theme such as "Commonwealth Studies." While such a theme would be in some senses "artificial," he insisted it would provide a focus for the college. Funt did not mention "Canadian Studies," but obviously it would provide a similar central thread.

The governance of the colleges was left to their own devices, except in terms of the all-important academic instruction and the reality that all officers were paid by the university. The result was a college resembling few other collegial systems widely recognized in the Western world. It would be too much to claim that the new St. John's College was unprecedented, but, as Anthony Waterman had pointed out, in academic terms the slate had been wiped clean. What St. John's College would become as it entered its next phase of life would be largely of its own making.

Chapter Ten

Seeking a New Identity, 1970–1980

THE FUTURE FOR ST. JOHN'S COLLEGE did not appear particularly bright in June 1970, as the college began life under the new agreement. Independent federal funding for the college had been withdrawn in 1967, the diocese had determined to train its ordinands elsewhere, and the university had taken over the college's teaching staff and direction of any teaching program it might house. The agreement of 1970 had been relatively hastily drafted, and it did not cover all contingencies. A protracted period would follow in which both parties would develop procedures and assert control over territory not spelled out in the agreement and would disagree over interpretation of what was spelled out. At first glance it appeared that the university had all the advantages in the game of working out the details of the agreement, but while the college's power had been reduced, it had not been totally eliminated, and it could gain back small accretions of territory over time by default. Although the university could win most of the biggest struggles over power, when battle lines were actually drawn, the default advantages of those actually in the college on a day-to-day basis were considerable. The college would thus unofficially over the years gain considerable administrative control over its own affairs and the space in its office/classroom building.

At the same time, those within the college quickly developed some sense of optimism for the future. St. John's certainly retained some assets, if it could work out a way to employ them positively. One asset was its buildings—including the residence, dining hall, and the chapel—to which the university obligingly added a new office and teaching wing completed in 1972. This addition to St. John's College was paid for out of University Grants Commission funds, with space in the building "for the use of the Faculty of Arts in co-operation with the College." Because the construction costs had run over budget, corners had been cut in the new wing, and, according to a report from the St. John's College Faculty Association in 1973, there were many complaints about it, especially lack of soundproofing, bad heating and cooling, and bad toilet fixtures. The windows did not open because sealed ones supposedly worked better with air conditioning, but the air conditioning in the building was intended to be—even when it was finally installed—a supplemental system, totally inadequate for the purpose. Many complained the building was an architectural monstrosity. In any event, the new teaching part of the buildings, and the administration of the library, were officially under the control of the university, but the residence, the chapel, and the space for the library remained firmly in the college's purview. Unfortunately, in the early 1970s, as had been the case for years, the residence and dining services were still losing money. On the other hand, the university was now responsible for the physical maintenance of the structure of the parts employed for teaching, relieving the college of a major concern. As often happens in shared space, that space not formally claimed and utilized by the external authority by default gradually in practice came under the aegis of the college, which was in practical occupation of it.

Another asset to St. John's was an administrative structure now financed by the university, although much of that structure was in its present form, now redundant or seemingly useless. In practice, the remaining college officers would have to find new things to do. The final advantage, probably the most important of all, was the presence of a young and energetic faculty membership that carried over from the days of the independent college and proceeded to add gradually to its numbers. This faculty membership understood that their classroom functions would be directed from outside the college, but also quickly realized that it would be possible to create a new extracurricular life for the institution, including a new system of governance. Warden Brown was not popular with many of the fellows, and opposition to his administration both energized the membership and gave it a sense of unity. As a result, a buoyant sense of promise characterized the thinking of most of the members of the college in the early years after the imposition of the new agreement. Willing and able to seize fleeting opportunities as well as to build on existing assets, the people of St. John's soon had the place humming in both old and new directions.

Whatever the new situation it was facing, the college found its student population much as it always had been. Statistics distributed in early 1971 indicated that a full 10 percent of students came from Kelvin High School, and another 30 percent from a small group of urban high schools and private schools: Vincent Massey, University of Winnipeg Collegiate, Grant Park, Miles Macdonell, St. John's-Ravenscourt, Silver Heights, Churchill, and Glenlawn. Another 20 percent came from other schools in the metropolitan Winnipeg area. The remainder came from outside the city, with the largest Manitoba contingents from Beausejour, Portage la Prairie, and Teulon. Forty-three students were from outside the province, nineteen from Saskatchewan. Only twenty students were from overseas, almost half from Hong Kong. As had long been the case, the students from beyond metropolitan Winnipeg made up a disproportionate number of those in residence. The college had a Rhodes Scholar (John Hutchings), and the sons of the current leaders of the provincial Liberal and Progressive Conservative parties were students at the same time.

The college in the 1970s had to deal with a number of major issues, more or less simultaneously, and with some minor but vexing ones as well. One of the major issues was the question of membership, both for faculty and for students. Given the fact that for both teachers and students, academic relationships were with university departments, how did one establish a voluntary relationship with the college, and what did it mean? This was as important a question for those living in the college residence as it was for those inhabiting the college's office space. Another was the matter of governance. The 1970 agreement had run roughshod over the old constitution and statutes of the college. Not only had the older Anglican traditions been sundered, but they would no longer suffice to govern members who did not have to be in the college because of their appointments but only because they wanted to be there. The college would have to be based on its faculty members, and a new, more democratic, structure seemed inevitable. A third area of concern was the relationship with the Anglican Church, damaged by a college failure to maintain good relations with diocese and alumni, and virtually shattered by the action of the diocese in withdrawing its educational mandate from St. John's. The restoration of the various historic connections would be a tricky business, involving the re-establishment of a divinity program, the founding of a chaplaincy presence in the college, and the creation of an alumni association. The college was fortunate throughout the 1970s to have the support, most of the time, of the Bishop of Rupert's Land, Barry Valentine. Finally among the major problems, there was the need to create what the agreement had called "a special area of interest" that would distinguish the college from other units on the campus. Among the less crucial but still important issues was the matter of the library, under the administrative control of the central library but still to be housed in the college. Also beginning to be recognized as valuable and in need of preservation were the college archives, one of the most extensive records of one of the oldest church-related institutions of higher learning in Canada. In addition, several more fleeting extra-collegiate items came temporarily to the fore, such as the location of the campus day-care centre and accommodation for Vietnamese boat people.

In a number of respects, the early post-agreement college was as far distant from the Anglican Church as it would ever be. The college was still reeling from the effects of its rejection by the synod in 1968 as the official theological college of the diocese, a decision confirmed by the synod in November 1970. This rejection had not simply caused but had somehow reflected a growing rift between the diocese and the college, possibly one begun during the Barfoot-Wilmot feud of the late 1950s. Certainly it was true that many parish clergy regarded those faculty in the college as favoured and spoiled in terms of workload and salary. Attendance at college chapel had reached a low ebb, except perhaps on Sunday morning, and was not likely to improve in the short run, since ordinands were no longer present at the college and the new warden was really not interested in music. At the same time, the bishop remained the chancellor of the college and the church was deeply embedded in the history and the statutes. On the other hand, as Anthony Waterman points out in his history of the chapel, Warden Brown did not employ the clergy of the college as a "chapter" and appeared to have had little real interest in the chapel as the symbolic centrepiece of the college. Peter Flynn remained chaplain of the college and Anglican chaplain of the university until 1972, but there was considerable trouble over the payment of his salary, particularly in view of cutbacks in university funding and an inability to use the income from trust funds for the chaplaincy. Funding a college chaplain out of college revenue would continue to be a contentious item, often solved by combining the chaplaincy with some other appointment, such as dean of residence.

In 1971, the college council was told by the finance committee that local businessmen opposed a capital campaign and recommended in the meantime the college "do what we can to improve public relations." The finance committee also suggested that the alumni be reorganized as a basic source of support, noting that nothing had been done with the alumni association for the past several years. In May 1971 the reorganization of the Friends of St. John's College Association was discussed in council, and by 1973 the warden was able to tell council that 260 of the 360 former members had renewed their membership, and that the association had raised over $6000 for the use of the college. Not until 1979 did a committee of council discuss the appointment of a development officer, which inevitably turned into the question of the desirability of a capital fund campaign. Many within the college were fearful of such a drive, partly because of the hostility of the diocese, and partly because to propose such fundraising would involve "consideration of arguments for the existence of St. John's College at the University of Manitoba." The college would remain resistant to major fundraising until the late 1980s.

Early in 1972, the college moved to raise the possibility of re-entering theological education. A subcommittee on theological education (chaired by Canon Brown) had been looking at preparing men for ordination. Since the college's theological program had been suspended in 1967, Brown reported in February, the university had added strong departments of religion and there were other resources available. The college had some funds, with an income of $1400 for theological prizes and other awards, "about which we do nothing at the moment." But there was no money available for an old-type seminary.

Any program would have to come from college funds. Brown asked whether the council had authority to proceed. He noted council had authorized suspension of the program, and the diocese had been consulted and accepted its reinstitution. The council thus moved to reactivate the program of preparing ordinands as from September 1972. By 1973 there would be a dozen ordinands enrolled in the college's divinity program. Only two students were full-time in theology. Most were intending to be worker-priests, ordained but in the secular workforce. Several from North Dakota were attending. This program was not welcomed with enthusiasm by everyone in the diocese. The same council meeting that moved to reactivation discussed a report of a committee on college-diocesan relations. This committee was one appointed by the diocese, and it was not very friendly. It pointed out that there would always be connections in constitutional terms, but added that the college was academically independent of the church and the diocese did not contribute to the finances of the college. The college was not limited to arts and sciences; it could have any program it wished so long as it funded it itself. In the past, Anglicans had contributed extensively to the college financially. According to the diocesan committee, the college's endowment in 1973 showed a total of $361,818, of which $259,443 was restricted and only $15,759 earmarked for theology. The committee concluded somewhat ominously that the diocese was the residual holder of the college assets if the college ever dissolved. Relations with the diocese would improve, however, under the bishopric of Barry Valentine, and the college made a real effort to involve members of the diocese in governance.

In 1975, V.B.H. Pellegrin, a member of the university psychology department who had been associated with the college since 1967, was appointed dean of divinity, and the first two ordinands from the new divinity program graduated at the 1977 convocation. Pellegrin worked hard to develop a distinctive program for divinity that would fill a niche and meet special needs within the Anglican Church. In April 1980 he reported on his Pastoral Skills Training by Extension Project. After two years of work, an extensive lay training curriculum entitled "Ministry and the People of God" had been prepared. It was directed to Anglican lay people who would like to become involved in pastoral ministry of the church. Work had begun, he added, on a second curriculum directed toward the needs of northern Christians (white and Aboriginal), called "Learning about Our Christian Ministry."

The maintenance of an Anglican presence at heavy financial expense was hard work, carried on against considerable opposition from secular elements within the college who felt that the money could be used more productively in other directions.

One of the thorniest problems facing the post-agreement college was the matter of membership, for both students and faculty alike. In the old days, one became a student of the college by enrolling in its courses, or a faculty member by receiving a teaching appointment. Registrar Marjorie Ward worried, in 1970, that fraternity and sorority memberships would dilute the identity of St. John's College students, although the real danger was that student allegiance would be transferred to the university. Those students living in the residence could legitimately still call themselves Johnians, but after 1970, students no longer took college courses (but university courses), and many no longer even took university courses that were taught in the college. Despite fears of loss of student loyalty, students continued to participate in campus activities, including intramural sports, as representatives of St. John's College. Those faculty occupying college offices were often assigned by the dean to the college, or invited by the warden, and were not necessarily interested in becoming members of it. In May 1971 George Baldwin at college council asserted that no one should occupy an office who had not been presented to council to become a member of the college. The warden responded that the space was arts space, and the assigning of faculty to St. John's was a "delicate business." The question kept being asked at council, but was never satisfactorily answered. One of the problems was that Warden Brown continued to invite university faculty to take up offices at the college without consultation, and these people gradually drove out of the faculty dining room those who regarded themselves as proper members of St. John's. The college council told the corporation in November 1972 that the issue remained unresolved. There was still difficulty in determining "the extent to which any of those teaching physically in St. John's College belongs to the University and/or to the College." The council favoured a more binding connection.

A year later, in November 1973, a preliminary report was made by a committee of the college board, chaired by Dean Mary Kinnear—the first female dean—appointed to develop criteria for college faculty membership in terms of mutual obligation. The committee had begun its work in the realization that there were no fixed criteria for membership in the college, although there was the 1969 college council precedent of a letter of appointment stating that appointments to the college would come either from applicants named by the college and accepted by the university, or from consenting members of the university faculty. The 1973 committee recommended two categories of membership: college fellow and visiting fellow. Initially, the notion was that a visiting fellow was one invited to the college for a specific field of study or who was a faculty member not participating in the life of the college. Later, college fellows became those who received financial remuneration above their university salaries, usually one dollar per year, while the visiting fellows were elected annually. Such fellows would not be full members of the college. This terminology seemed to meet the need for labels that would treat the faculty within the college as volunteers in its affairs rather than as paid employees. It was entrenched in the subsequent reforms of college governance and the subsequent revisions of the statutes, which made the fellows the basis of the enterprise and allowed them, through assembly, to control additions to their numbers.

Of a series of difficult problems facing the college after the agreement, easily the most intractable was the question of how the institution was to be governed. According to the 1957 statutes, the college was owned and operated, in the first instance, by a college corporation, headed by the chancellor and including the major officers of the college. The corporation in turn appointed the college council, which dealt with most business and academic matters of the college. The president and secretary of the faculty association served on the council, but it consisted mostly of college officers and various representatives of the church. In addition there was a college board, consisting of the warden and all faculty at the rank of associate professor or above, which dealt with academic discipline and academic standing, as well as recommendations for the appointment of resident fellows (who "shall ordinarily reside in the College and take such teaching work as is assigned to them while engaged in research in the higher branches of their Department under the direction of the Professors in the Department in St. John's College or in the University of Manitoba.") and for the award of scholarships and prizes. It had met infrequently.

Almost everyone within the college agreed virtually from the outset, some tacitly and some actively, that the new college would have to be built upon its volunteer membership, those faculty members whose academic responsibilities were elsewhere and who could not be coerced in any formal or overt way. Obviously the system that would work best was one that would turn the faculty membership into the principal governing body of the college, as had happened informally both immediately before and after the imposition of the new agreement. Not everyone involved with the college agreed with the concept of an institution democratically governed principally by its members, and, more to the point, finding a satisfactory model for such an institution was no easy matter, since none of the obvious places to turn were very democratic in their governance. The Anglican Church itself was a top-down hierarchical institution that had rejected government by parishioners when it had driven out the Puritans in the sixteenth and seventeenth centuries. The university was another hierarchical institution that had discouraged democracy as much as possible, at least above the departmental level. The University of Manitoba departments, the basic building blocks of the system, were in the 1970s still formally administered by heads appointed from above, although in practice some departments had introduced participatory democracy. In any case, academic departments were not a very useful model for a college, any more than were most downtown business corporations, although a large law firm with multiple partners might have served fairly usefully as a precedent. For some reason, it did not occur to most of those involved to turn to voluntary organizations for acceptable models

By 1972 most parties were agreed that the 1957 statutes must be redone because they were based on conditions that no longer existed. At a corporation meeting on 2 November 1972, Mr. Richard Shead of the finance committee commented that the problems were procedural, mechanical, and constitutional, and that a committee needed to be struck to study the statutes and revise them. At the subsequent council meeting, the nominating committee filled the standing committees: finance, and administration and staff. The administration and staff committee no longer could function as originally designed but by statute it had to have members, which the nominating committee hoped could "make its contribution in other directions." As for the college board, it was supposed to consist of associate and full professors, but had already agreed to add faculty members at a lower rank. At its last meeting, the board had moved that its membership be extended to make it more representative of college faculty: "until the College Statutes are amended it would strengthen the College Board for Faculty Members of the College to elect to the Board three members below the rank of Associate Professor and that the Student Body elect two additional members from the student members of the College." This request was brought to council and accepted. Early in 1973 the bishop reported to council that he would appoint a committee to work on the statutes, and the synod subsequently agreed to support the principle of revision. As a result, in 1974 the bishop appointed a wide-ranging committee to prepare a major revision to the statutes. A preliminary draft of that revision was circulated in the autumn of 1974, and as revised became part of the "Report on the Future of St. John's College," which was completed in March 1975 and widely discussed around the college.

This report redefined the purposes of the college:

> In following the purposes of Archbishop Machray, St. John's College aims to promote intellectual excellence in a context of Christian perceptions about God, the world and man. The College expects to develop and cherish in all its members rigorous intellectual discipline, sound moral integrity and commitment to the service of others. It pursues these same qualities in training candidates for the priesthood of the church. The College strives to be a vital centre of scholarly activity within the Canadian academic community as well as being an intellectual and spiritual focus of the Anglican Church in Rupert's Land.

It then recommended two governing bodies. One would be the present corporation, reduced substantially in size, consisting of the chancellor, six members elected by the synod, and six members elected by a new body called assembly, the product of the amalgamation of the present council and the present college board (of which at least one would be a college fellow, one a student, and one a member of the Friends of St. John's). The corporation would carry out most of the functions of the previous corporation. It would have the power to manage the business and property of the college, to borrow money, and to negotiate financial matters with the university. The assembly would be managed by an executive committee of six, consisting of the chairman of assembly, the warden, and four other members elected by assembly. Assembly would have three standing committees: the administrative committee, a student affairs committee, and a program planning and development committee. Each would meet monthly and report to assembly. Each would present recommendations to assembly for approval and implementation. College budgets would be generated by the administrative committee and submitted to assembly. The warden served ex-officio on all committees and had "overall responsibility for the academic, administrative and pastoral life of the College."

Much criticism of these proposals emerged from traditionalists, one of the most articulate coming from prominent Anglican layman J. Keith Knox, dated 4 October 1974. Knox insisted that adequate attention had not been paid in the draft to "the group to which it [the college] looks for financial and other support." He also argued that assembly had too much budgetary power and the corporation too little, since the latter had "no input, save as vicariously through the Assembly, [in] any budgetary and other revenue matters." Knox insisted that the college corporation appointed the auditors and ought to have approval of the budget. He worried that the powers given to the warden were not sufficiently explicit, leaving him in a position where his popularity with the members of assembly would be a paramount consideration. He objected to the inclusion of the bursar and the registrar in assembly. Overall, Knox feared that "the influence of the Anglican Church and its community on the day-to-day operations of the College, as well as on policy and administrative matters, will be much reduced and, indeed, may be minimal or non-existent." What he saw was a college in which all powers "save those of guardians of the physical assets of the College," were in the hands of the college assembly, which—although he did not spell out the point—was chiefly controlled by the fellows. It was in some ways a curious response, given that the college had been virtually abandoned by the diocese, but those who liked the notion of an Anglican St. John's College liked it a lot. In a written response to the Knox critique, Francis Carroll, still a retired fellow of the college, argued that the basic relationships of the faculty with college administration, council, and corporation were all being misunderstood. The faculty were not employees of the college, and had to be actively involved in its deliberations if the whole enterprise were to succeed. As for not putting control in the hands of those who provided the financial support, Carroll emphasized that church, corporation, and council did not provide the college with regular revenue. The church merited a voice in governance for historical reasons, but not for financial ones, wrote Carroll. In January 1976 the first organizational meeting of the college assembly was held, but the revision of the statutes to make its existence legal dragged on for a number of years, since many outside the college had objections to various aspects of the proposed new system of government. Council continued in operation under the chairmanship of Bishop Valentine until 1979, when he stepped down for personal reasons. Valentine had been initially responsible for drafting the new statutes, and he was replaced in this capacity by Professor Arthur Braid of the faculty of law. In November of that year, chair of the administration committee (and first chair of assembly) Phyllis Hutchinson—who was an Anglican layperson—pointed out that as a result of the 1970 agreement, the college now received substantial public monies. The college budget had three areas: university budget, internal college budget, and faculty of divinity budget; the college had no voice in the library budget. At the same time, no corresponding change in the structure of college governance had enabled any one body to oversee these financial components. This was a gap that needed to be addressed as soon as possible. A few months later, Professor Braid reported that in council there were difficulties in drafting the new statutes. Under the new draft the warden would have no power. Braid saw the new statutes as paralleling the university structure, with the corporation as board of governors, the assembly as senate, and the warden as the dean's council. Mrs. Hutchinson noted that the philosophy of the college had changed since the first drafting, and that members of assembly needed to be consulted. Braid said he was not drafting on behalf of the assembly but on behalf of the bishop. He refused to consult with assembly but only with the warden in the matter. This incident suggested some of the nature of the continuing problems over the statutes.

From the release of the Funt Report, if not before, the leadership of St. John's College was aware that most teaching responsibility was to be moved from the college to the departments, although the college would be encouraged to continue its own "special area of interest." The special area that most appealed to many members of the college at the end of the 1960s was Canadian studies. Votes at this time about Canadian studies were overwhelmingly in favour. For some years dating back to the 1950s, the college attempted to emphasize the teaching of Canadian subjects in history and English, and it was a natural step now to attempt to take advantage of the upsurge—both national and local—of concern for Canadian content in teaching, especially in arts and social science courses. From the beginning, however, Canadian studies proved a difficult— almost impossible—horse to ride successfully, chiefly because the movement meant very different things to different people, and it was impossible to fix on a single standard definition.

As the Canadian universities had expanded during the decade of the 1960s, they had found that one of their greatest problems was in finding qualified faculty to teach the increased number of students in the increased number of institutions of higher education in the country. University expansion did not involve simply the creation of new universities, although a number were begun, particularly in Ontario and British Columbia, but an enormous increase in the student bodies of existing universities, such as the University of Manitoba. For a few brief years, Canadian universities hired large numbers of new faculty, mainly recently graduated Ph.D.'s, wherever they could find them. Canadian graduate schools could hardly begin to meet the demand. Many of the newcomers came from British universities, a few from other universities in the Commonwealth, but the largest number came from the American graduate schools, which were turning out people with completed doctorates at a considerable rate, mainly in response to the scare over the "brain gap" highlighted by the Russian scientific successes of the late 1950s, including Sputnik. Because of their numbers, these American recruits were feared to be particularly hard to assimilate into Canadian university curricula in the arts and social sciences. They had no familiarity with Canadian culture or Canadian society, and, when they taught in the introductory courses in their disciplines, relied on American textbooks and American material almost exclusively. These fears proved greatly exaggerated, and most of the American academics gradually became totally Canadianized, although in some fields in some universities at the end of the 1960s, Canadian content virtually disappeared. But if course content sometimes became increasingly Americanized in the later 1960s, this development was countered by a simultaneous rise in Canadian nationalism among students. The result was a vocal demand for Canadian content in the classroom, a demand that provided much of the popular impetus for the emergence of "Canadian studies" at the time. A virtual explosion of books—textbooks and more specialized works—arose to meet the new need, and for a few years publishers vied with one another to publish Canadian material. Canadian studies programs expanded right across the nation. By 1971 there were twenty-two programs in Canadian universities.

While Canadian studies programs briefly flourished and proliferated in the early 1970s, the formal movement was unable to sustain its momentum. Partly this was because Canadian content was rapidly introduced into most teaching in most departments, which resolved the needs of many who had supported Canadian studies, and partly because there was no agreement on how to define Canadian studies or how to fit it into the existing departmental structures. Many in the life sciences insisted that all their work was by definition Canadian, since they dealt with the health of the Canadian people, while other natural scientists maintained that nothing they worked with could be labelled distinctly Canadian. In some arts fields, such as philosophy, music, and literature, traditional critics maintained that little that was Canadian was worth studying. The influential first volume of a report on Canadian studies in 1975 authored by Tom Symons (*To Know Ourselves: The Report of the Commission of Canadian Studies,* commissioned and published by the Association of Universities and Colleges of Canada) epitomized the nature of much of the confusion. While in his report Symons acknowledged the possibility of an area-studies or interdisciplinary approach, most readers were likely to take from his discipline-by-discipline discussions the view that Canadian content was to be equated with Canadian studies.

In the months before the agreement was finalized, St. John's College had moved to attempt to establish Canadian studies as its "special area of interest." The college council on 17 March 1970 approved the establishment of a Canadian studies program, and George Baldwin, the chairman of the Canadian studies committee, prepared a budget calling for an annual expenditure of $38,750, which he forwarded to the chairman of the college council. Various attempts to persuade the dean of arts to recognize St. John's as the centre of Canadian studies on the campus met with little success. On 9 February 1971, the college council was told that while former Dean of Arts Lloyd Dulmage had supported the college in its quest for a Canadian studies centre, Dean Robert McCarthy insisted that Arts had made no commitment to the proposal, which had not been approved by senate. More than a year after the agreement, on 22 October 1971, a faculty committee of the college proposed again that approval of department heads and the dean of arts be once again sought for participation of a number of departments in a "Department of Canadian Studies" at the college as the college's "area of emphasis." Departments to be involved were anthropology, economics, English, geography, history, philosophy, political studies, religion, Romance languages, and sociology. This "department" was subsequently called a "Centre for Canadian Studies" by the college, and its institution was expected to "provide a general focus and unifying purpose . . . to St. John's College." It was never formally embodied by the university administration, however.

In October 1976, Warden Brown sent a letter to Dr. D.R. Campbell, president of the university, in response to queries by the university's board of governors about the Symons report and the status of Canadian studies at the university. The letter had been drafted by Dean of Studies Francis Carroll in consultation with Warden Brown. It noted a report presented in early 1970 to college faculty and council that recommended a Canadian studies centre be created at the University of Manitoba and located at the college. This report wanted an interdisciplinary academic program and a supplemental program to interest public and students in Canadian affairs, wrote Brown. The college had been only partially successful in realizing its ambitions, he added. University departments had been willing to pay attention to Canadian courses in their disciplines and to teach some of them at the college, as well as participating in some form of interdisciplinary approach to Canadian studies. The university had made it possible for its students to have majors and minors and honours in Canadian studies. But the creation of a centre at St. John's College had not been realized, and Canadian studies as a formal discipline had not flourished at the college, the members of which devoted the bulk of their energies to supplemental programs of public events and professional/scholarly activities. Some of those events had been extremely popular. Debate on the Gray Report on Canadian investment between Dean Ruben Bellan and economist Cy Gonick in late 1971, for example, had to be moved from the college to the multi-purpose room at University Centre, where between 700 and 1000 persons attended.

Despite lack of budget, the college had held public discussions on Canadian topics and organized several conferences that were truly interdisciplinary. A Canadian art collection had been begun, chiefly by Professor Ken Hughes (soon to become chairman of the Manitoba Arts Council), who used a small discretionary fund and the power of persuasion to great effect. The process of covering the college's walls with contemporary Canadian art, most of it produced by local artists, was already well underway. Most of the art was donated. The *Journal of Canadian Fiction* had office space at the college, as had the journal *CV II* (edited by the poet Dorothy Livesay, who subsequently offered her papers to the college). Birk Sproxton and Wayne Tefs edited *The Sphinx: A Magazine of Literature and Society* from the college. Turnstone Press had been recently founded, partly by St. John's faculty, and had produced four volumes of poetry over the summer of 1976. Prof. John Mathiasson had founded an anthropological society called Association for the Study of the Peoples of Manitoba. St. John's College had funded these projects on a shoestring and could use a budget for them, Brown insisted. His letter to President Campbell noted other evidence of Canadian studies interest at the college. It had expanded Canadian holdings in the library. Moreover, St. John's College in 1970 had a resident faculty of twenty-one, of whom three were Canadian specialists, while six years later it had thirty-three resident faculty, with fourteen lecturing in Canadian topics. The college still wanted to have a Canadian studies centre in 1976. If that were unacceptable, said the letter, it sought a Canadian studies board of two members from St. John's College, two from St. Paul's, and two from the faculty of arts, to manage the Canadian studies academic program at the university. Nothing ever came of this initiative.

As the college's correspondence with the university demonstrated, throughout the 1970s and early 1980s it found extremely frustrating the refusal of the parent institution to come to terms with what many university administrators labelled the college's "self-designated" interest in Canadian studies. It was never entirely clear why the university adopted such an attitude, although apparently too many vested interests across the campus opposed allowing the college to entrench its position. At the same time, as the correspondence also suggested, the college had informally found Canadian studies a suitable medium for focussing much of its non-curricular energies. Specialists in matters Canadian did congregate at St. John's, and their shared concerns did lead to congeniality and collegiality. Given the ways in which formal Canadian studies programs gradually shrivelled away across the nation, the college's informal focus was very likely a better direction for the future, since it required continual innovation and would not harden into fixed administrative patterns.

As it became increasingly clear that the university would not centralize Canadian studies at the college, efforts were begun to develop other distinctive academic programs there. In autumn of 1976 Bishop Valentine formed a group to brainstorm about the college. It met over the next few months and produced a "Report to the Bishop's Committee for the Development of St. John's College." The principal recommendation was that, beginning in September 1977, each incoming student to St. John's would get a faculty advisor, who would supervise the student throughout his or her university career. This scheme foundered for want of interest among either students or faculty. The Valentine Committee also suggested the development of college exchange programs.

The willingness to consider programs besides Canadian Studies did not mean that the college abandoned its original interests, although circumstances often ran against it. In 1979, for example, it agreed to provide space for the Selkirk Papers, a major editorial project to edit and publish all the papers of Lord Selkirk—the founder of Manitoba—in a series of twelve letterpress volumes. The project was fully supported by the university and the provincial government, and hoped to get most of its $5-million budget from the Major Editorial Grants Program of the Social Sciences and Humanities Research Council. As part of the proposal, in 1980 the author was brought to the university and housed at St. John's College.

The library was an ongoing concern for the college after the agreement, chiefly because that document did not really spell out in any detail the nature of the relationship between the college and the university regarding its administration. The university was to fund and administer the library, but the library remained physically within the college's space, and consisted chiefly of the college's books, accumulated over a number of years. By 1970 the library was clearly short of space, both for student study and for storage of additional volumes, and the university was not particularly interested in any sort of expansion or improvement to the facilities. Some in the college feared that physical conditions were part of the reason for the difficulty in finding a new librarian. Opinion was sharply divided between those who wanted to mount a major expansion, involving new construction, and those who sought to make more space within the existing structure.

In July 1971, Arthur Millward was appointed as college librarian, paid by the university. Millward was an Anglican priest who had left pastoral work. He and the warden extended the library into seminar room L over the summer of 1972, admittedly without council approval, as a pre-emptive strike to minimize the need for extensive expansion.

The library was the subject of considerable debate in council in late 1973, when George Baldwin chaired a committee that recommended library expansion, a building fund to finance it, and a priority system for book purchase that would meet the college's interests in divinity and Canadian studies. Discussion disclosed that no one knew at present how many students used the library, or for what purposes. Everyone agreed that the library was the heart of the academic function and nobody wanted books culled out or put in storage. Nothing was done about the library at this point, for the recommendations were turned aside by the head of the university library, but two years later council approved further expansion into the next adjoining room on the third floor of the old college building. In 1980 Arthur Millward reported that the library no longer served a "coherent academic body." The college had focussed on Canadian studies and emphasized Canadian literature. In theology, material in biblical studies had been collected. There was much emphasis on history, economics, and sociology. Over the past year the college library had added a photocopier (transferred from the medical library) and a microfiche reader, while the college circulation system was being integrated with the other campus libraries. Holdings in 1978–79 were 37,738 volumes and in 1979–80 were 38,710 volumes. Circulation in 1978–79 was 12,519 items and in 1979–80 was 11,751 items. The college was unable to stop integration into the larger campus system, but was in the 1990s able to invoke the agreement in order to prevent services from being reduced.

In April 1980, Warden Jim Brown stepped down from his post. A search committee for a new warden reported to council that it had sent letters to all heads of Anglican colleges in Canada and the US, and advertised in scholarly and Anglican publications. There were thirty applications for the position, ten of which were withdrawn before the search committee began its deliberations. One of the candidates was the Reverend Murdith McLean, a Johnian whose great-grandfather had been the original warden of the college, who was an administrator at Red Deer College. He was quickly selected, and a new regime would begin in the autumn of 1980. By the time McLean took office, many of the transitional problems resulting from the introduction of the 1970 agreement had been more or less resolved, although statutory revision continued to bedevil the college for several more years. Nevertheless, the college was a work still very much in progress. St. John's entered the 1980s a much different institution from the one that had begun the 1970s. Hopes remained high that somehow or another the university would come to recognize the value of colleges to the academic enterprise at the University of Manitoba, and would find some fresh utility for St. John's College.

Epilogue

1980–2005

MURDITH MCLEAN WAS FORMALLY INSTALLED AS WARDEN in the St. John's College chapel on 21 September 1980. This was the first time that such an installation had ever occurred in the chapel, and marked, in a sense, a re-dedication of both the chapel and the college to their original purposes. The service, designed for the occasion, was modelled on that for the induction and institution of a parochial incumbent, with the ceremonial modified to fit the circumstances of a church college. The sermon on that occasion was preached by Anthony Waterman, who began by emphasizing that St. John's College was an integral part of both the University of Manitoba and of the church in the Province of Rupert's Land. The preacher went on to point out that the new warden had to thread his way between several alternative scenarios. On the one hand, many had "hinted darkly at winding up the Agreement, selling the buildings, leaving the campus, and using the assets of the Corporation to set up some purely diocesan institution." On the other hand, "free-thinking enthusiasts on the Faculty, having sought in vain to understand what, if anything, the Anglican Church desires or deserves of its college, have tried to cut the Gordian knot by turning it into an Institute for Australian literature or a centre of Manitoba Studies." Waterman counselled resistance to both these extremities, and, indeed, the history of the past twenty-five years of the college has seen neither of them emerge as dominant. Instead, the college has continued to search, with various degrees of success, for ways to serve both the academic community and the church.

Over the past quarter-century, a number of initiatives have occurred on the academic side, some of them more successful than others. One that definitely worked was the establishment of the Ward Lectures. When Registrar Marjorie Ward—who had held the college together administratively since its days on Broadway—had retired at the end of the 1970s, the college established a distinguished Canadian lecture series in her honour. The first speaker was former faculty member William S. Pickering in 1981. The second speaker was Tom Symons, and he was followed by a series of important figures in various aspects of Canadian cultural activity. The Ward Lecture remains an important date on the calendar of anyone interested in the future of Canadian culture.

In some ways the most fruitful academic initiative, spearheaded by Warden McLean, was the recruitment of outstanding scholars, mainly from the arts faculty, but including one from music (Lawrence Ritchey), as senior fellows, to join an already distinguished collection of existing fellows. McLean recalls being accused by University of Manitoba administrators of open raids on the arts departments for talent. Many of the new fellows had already established reputations in various aspects of Canadian studies. Apart from the fellows specializing in Canadian literature, however, the college seemed to have considerable difficulty in drawing the attention of both the academic and general community to the very real distinction of the faculty housed there.

In the early 1980s the college, with the active support of new warden Murdith McLean, did establish an interdisciplinary arrangement whereby an elite group of incoming students could elect to take most of their courses at the college and would work together as a special coordinated cadre inside and outside the classroom. Despite extensive recruiting efforts by Director Martin Gerwin, however, this program (called the associateship program) was never able to attract sufficient numbers of incoming students or sufficient outside funding (from the university or the community) to become viable, and it gradually faded away. More successful was the establishment of an exchange arrangement for students and faculty with a college in Tasmania and another program for academic exchange with Germany.

On the Canadian studies front, the record was mixed. Over the years, the college continued the sponsorship of regular conferences in Canadian studies. Unfortunately, the grants program at the Social Sciences and Humanities Research Council had its funding terminated just as the Selkirk Project in 1981 completed its extensive application, and the hoped-for money never became available. The project brought out two volumes of the writings of Lord Selkirk under the auspices of the Manitoba Record Society, which for many years was housed at the college. Later, in 1983, the college participated fully in the deliberations of a university committee appointed by the president, chaired by Ken Osborne of the faculty of education, which ended up calling for the expenditure of $100,000 to appoint a full-time director of Canadian studies and establish a proper program. Whether the college would have become the site of the recommended centre of Canadian studies was never determined, but, in the end, the money was not authorized by the university senate. An effort by an assembly review committee in 1991 failed to create a "Research Centre for Canadian Studies" as a way to package publicly the very real resources of the college in this area of study. In some ways the failure of these major initiatives may have made possible, through the efforts of Dean of Studies Kathryn Young at the end of the century, the eventual location of a small formal program of Canadian studies at the college.

On another more positive front, a small group of "concerned members" of the college spearheaded by Fellow Angela Davis, a distinguished art historian, met on 4 February 1987 to see about better housing for the college archives material, then being kept in the old wing of alumni secretary

Irene Carter's office. Some work had been done on organizing the archival material by students in 1984, 1985, and 1987, but the records were basically in a disorganized state. Despite an assembly motion on 22 May 1987 that the college donate its archives to the provincial archives by July 1987, nothing was done for some time; the ecclesiastical archivist and the general synod archivist were both hostile to the transfer because the provincial archives insisted that ownership of the records had to be ceded to them before full archival services could be provided. The archives committee met regularly on this matter for several years, and in November 1992 recommended the transfer of the records to the University of Manitoba Archives on the grounds that the university was residual "owner" of the records. The transfer was agreed to in early 1993, but the processing of the material was not begun until 1998, when $18,000 was raised to produce a guide to the records. Laurie Wilmot was responsible for a large portion of the fundraising. The bulk of the project was completed by 2000, although most of the post-1980 material was neither transferred to the archives nor processed. The strength of these archives as an historical record of both the college and the university is considerable.

On the theological side, for most of the remainder of the century, St. John's would concentrate its theological education on older lay people and the Aboriginal community, with a constantly declining number of faculty members, until John Stafford, a new dean of the faculty of theology (the name change from the faculty of divinity was important) would attempt to find a new place for the old divinity school. The result was the mounting of an accessible program of biblical and theological learning at the undergraduate and graduate level. Courses could be taken for personal enrichment as well as for preparation for various ministries within the diocese, and the faculty encouraged a collaborative relationship with other institutions within and without Winnipeg. Efforts by Murdith McLean and his successor, Janet Hoskins—who became in 1997 acting warden, in 1998 interim warden, and in 1999 both its first regularly appointed lay warden and its first regularly appointed female warden*—attempted to bring the diocese into a closer relationship with the

---

* Mary Kinnear served as acting warden in 1992-93.

college, and a number of Anglicans both lay and clerical presently sit on college council.

For all those attending St. John's College, in secular or theological programs, a major improvement since 1980 has occurred in the amount of financial aid available to students in the form of bursaries and grants. By 2005, the amount of money available to college students exceeded $60,000.

In many ways, perhaps the outstanding development of the past twenty-five years has been the establishment of a regular fundraising system for the college. When he was acting warden in 1986, Francis Carroll had raised the possibility of a regular fundraising arrangement. In October 1989, the college approached Community Charitable Counselling Service of Canada, Inc. (cccs) in Toronto to conduct a feasibility study for a proposed capital campaign. This followed meetings between Murdith McLean and cccs in August and September 1989. The study was carried out between October and December 1989. It consisted of a questionnaire of thirty questions, on which interviews were based. Internally, eight faculty, two staff, seven members of council, and seven students were interviewed. Externally, two alumni, seven clergy, ten members of the Anglican community, eight leaders of business and industry, three administrators from the University of Manitoba, and one foundation member were interviewed. The total of fifty-five was considerably less than originally intended, because of difficulties in meeting with outside respondents. The main questions to be asked involved the level of approval for fundraising and the level of financial support. The respondents were fairly evenly split regarding their perception of the college: 36 percent thought it above average, 34 percent thought it average or below, and 29 percent had no opinion. The biggest weakness was perceived to be the quality of the physical plant (83 percent gave the plant a 3 or less on a scale of 5). The high number of no opinions was interpreted as representing a lack of profile.

Among the various priorities suggested by the college (new library, endowments for academic progress and scholarships, great hall, professorial chair in Western Canadian studies, residence renovation, lectureship in

Anglican history and theology, handicapped access), the residence and the great hall got the most favourable responses, and Canadian studies, followed by Anglican projects and handicapped access, received the least favourable responses. A number of respondents wanted to convert the chapel to either a library or a great hall. The study concluded that "the overall perception of the purpose of the institution is oblique," but that most people favoured a campaign, with a goal of $1 million to $1.5 million was deemed to be feasible. It recommended a better focussed case and the conversion of the chapel to other purposes (with the construction of a much smaller chapel).

In 1991, in the midst of discussions over fundraising, the college received a report from yet another review committee, this one appointed by assembly in 1989 and consisting chiefly of fellows (Margaret Allen, David Arnason, Julie Baker, Francis Carroll, Dawne McCance) under the chairmanship of Robert Thomas, and with ex-officio input from Dr. Charles Jago, principal of Huron College, who was visiting the university to do an external review of University College. This document provides us with an in-house progress report on the college ten years into the McLean wardenship. This committee began its report by emphasizing that, for the most part, the college seemed unable to present itself to its various publics (with the possible exceptions of the diocese and the university). There was some suggestion that the college did not even present itself well to some of its own members (retired fellows and junior fellows, for example). The need for a mission statement against which the college could measure itself was stressed. Such a statement was subsequently produced. It read:

> The mission of St. John's College, as a founding and member College of the University of Manitoba, is to foster community, informed by Anglican tradition, in which students, fellows and staff, working in varied disciplines and programs, are brought together in an intimate, humane and supportive environment. By this means, the College aims to provide a rich and well-srounded educational experience for its members and to promote excellence in theological and secular learning.

The report noted that the residence, while popular with students, had been allowed to run down through lack of maintenance. This was, of course, a real argument for a fundraising campaign, as was the deteriorating physical condition of the library and the general fabric of the college. A fair proportion of the funds raised by the fundraising campaign were put into residence renovation and upgrading.

After much debate over the question of whether to hire professional fundraisers or use its own fundraisers, the council decided to proceed, with its own fundraising structure. The campaign, to be called "Founding the Future," started early in 1992 with fundraising among the college faculty and staff, under the chairmanship of Francis Carroll. The initial goal was $2 million, later scaled back to $1 million as more realistic. The honourary chairs of the campaign proper were prominent lawyer Lorne Campbell and former premier Duff Roblin. The campaign co-chairs were John Deacon and Laurie Wilmot. "Funding the Future" was declared successfully completed in 1996, with over $1 million raised. Among its legacies was a permanent fundraising office and officer, as well as constantly improving relations with the college's thousands of alumni.

In 2003, the University of Manitoba Press relocated to the college, thus returning to an earlier somewhat lapsed tradition of the 1970s that saw a number of presses and cultural organizations being housed within the walls of St. John's.

What direction the college will take in the future is quite unclear. It is clear that St. John's remains underfunded. It remains equally clear that the college remains underappreciated in the larger community. Few people in Winnipeg or in Manitoba seem to be aware of the academic distinction of the college's faculty or of the college's contribution to the life of the mind on the banks of the Red River. What we can safely say, however, paraphrasing the words of a popular Broadway song, is "WE'RE STILL HERE!"

A Note on Sources

The vast bulk of the documentation for this history is to be found in the St. John's College archives, on deposit in the Archives and Special Collections of the University of Manitoba. A guide to these archives is to be found in Joan Kennedy, compiler, "A User's Guide to the St. John's College Archives." Most particularly useful were the minutes of College Council and the various runs of student magazines and newspapers. Also helpful were the annual reports of the Synod of Rupert's Land, held at the Archives of the Synod in Winnipeg. Four published works were invaluable: William Fraser's *A History of St. John's College, Winnipeg, 1866-1966* (Winnipeg, 1966); Robert Machray's *Life of Robert Machray* (Toronto, 1909); George A. Wells's memoir, published as *The Fighting Bishop* (Toronto, 1971); and Laurence Wilmot, *The St. John's College Story: A Documentary* (Winnipeg, 2002). The biography of Bishop Machray takes on unusual value since its author, the bishop's nephew, destroyed all of the bishop's papers on which it was based when he was finished writing it. I am also indebted to a number of "native informants," college fellows and employees who have been part of the ongoing story over the past forty years. Anthony Waterman's recollections have been particularly useful, as have George Baldwin's memories and saved files. In addition, I have benefited from the memories and advice of David Arnason, Francis Carroll, Mary Kinnear, Derek McLean, Murdith McLean, and Kathryn Young

Photo Credits

Unless indicated otherwise, all photographs are reproduced courtesy of the Archives and Special Collections, University of Manitoba (St. John's College Collection). The archival objects appearing at the beginning of each chapter have been reproduced courtesy of St. John's College.